UNDERSTA
FUNDAMI
AND
EVANGELICAL.

Understanding Fundamentalism and Evangelicalism

George M. Marsden

WILLIAM B. EERDMANS PUBLISHING COMPANY
GRAND RAPIDS, MICHIGAN

Copyright © 1991 by Wm. B. Eerdmans Publishing Co.
255 Jefferson Ave. S.E., Grand Rapids, Mich. 49503

Printed in the United States of America

09 08 07 06 05 04 03   13 12 11 10 9 8 7

Library of Congress Cataloging-in-Publication Data

Marsden, George M., 1939 –
    Understanding fundamentalism and evangelicalism /
George M. Marsden.
        p.   cm.
    ISBN 0-8028-0539-6
    1. Fundamentalism — History.   2. Evangelicalism — United
States — History.   3. Machen, J. Gresham (John Gresham),
1881 – 1937.
    I. Title.
    BT82.2.M39   1991
    277.3'082 — dc20   90-22212
                                                           CIP

Contents

CONTENTS

Preface

THIS BOOK PROVIDES an overview of the history of American fundamentalism and evangelicalism plus interpretations of some important themes. It is designed for readers who are seeking either a brief introduction to these topics or some deeper analysis, or both. It is thus meant to be suitable as a supplement text for colleges, seminaries, or church study groups where these topics are being considered.

Although each chapter has been edited to fit this volume, this book developed largely from a series of essays written during the 1980s. At the beginning of that decade I published *Fundamentalism and American Culture: The Shaping of Twentieth-Century Evangelicalism, 1870-1925* (New York: Oxford University Press, 1980). That book coincided with the reemergence of fundamentalism as a conspicuous force in American life. During the next years I was asked to elaborate on themes in the *Fundamentalism* volume, particularly as they shed light on recent developments. This book collects some of those reflections.

Unlike most books of essays, however, this collection includes a narrative survey of the subject as well as analysis of particular themes. The majority of this narrative comes from a section of *Eerdmans' Handbook to Christianity in America* on American Christianity from 1870 to 1930 that I have adapted to be a survey of the crisis that hit Protestantism during that era and the rise of fundamentalism. This is supplemented by a second essay surveying the attempt, especially among the heirs to the original fundamentalism, to build a new evangelical coalition in the era since the 1930s. This latter survey drew on material from a second major study, *Reforming Fundamentalism: Fuller Seminary and the New Evangelicalism* (Grand Rapids: Eerdmans, 1987). In that volume, as in the current one, I looked primarily at people who called themselves "evangelicals," many of whom had strong ties to earlier fundamentalism. As the Introduction that follows explains, evangelicalism can be used in a much more inclusive way. This volume sketches the background of such broader evangelicalism but does not presume to offer deep understanding of its many varieties and aspects. Rather, its focus is on fundamentalists and on the sort of self-styled "evangelicals" who typically had fundamentalist backgrounds.

In offering interpretations of these traditions I have looked mainly at two themes of controversy with the larger culture: politics and views of science. At the time of the first advent of fundamentalism during the 1920s, no theme was more prominent than its view of science, especially biological evolution. In more recent fundamentalism, its political stand drew most attention. In dealing with each of these themes, I attempt to relate the distinctive views of fundamentalists to the nineteenth-century evangelical claims to stand for universal and self-evident cultural principles.

The one other topic I have included focuses on one fundamentalist leader, J. Gresham Machen. Machen was not a typical figure, but he was a pivotal one, especially for the sort of evangelical who reads serious books. Since Machen remains highly controversial, understanding him necessarily raises important questions concerning evaluation. Hence I have used this essay as a way of raising broader evaluative issues concerning fundamentalist and evangelical critiques of modernity.

Acknowledgments

The chapters in this volume appeared in earlier versions in the following volumes:

Chapter One: Adapted from *Eerdmans' Handbook to Christianity in America,* edited by Mark A. Noll, Nathan O. Hatch, George M. Marsden, David F. Wells, and John D. Woodbridge (Grand Rapids: William B. Eerdmans Publishing Company, 1983).

Chapter Two: Adapted from "Unity and Diversity in the Evangelical Resurgence," in David W. Lotz, et al., eds., *Altered Landscapes: Christianity in America, 1935–1985* (William B. Eerdmans Publishing Company, 1989).

Chapter Three: Adapted from "Afterword," in Mark A. Noll, ed., *Religion and American Politics: From the Colonial Period to the 1980s* (New York: Oxford University Press, 1989). Copyright © 1989 by Oxford University Press, Inc. Reprinted by permission.

Chapter Four: Adapted from "Preachers of Paradox," in Mary Douglas and Steven Tipton, eds., *Religion and America: Spirituality in a Secular Age* (Boston: Beacon Press, 1983). Copyright

ACKNOWLEDGMENTS

Chapter Five: Adapted and reprinted from "Evangelicals and the Scientific Culture," in Michael J. Lacy, ed., *Religion & Twentieth Century American Intellectual Life* (Cambridge, Eng.: Woodrow Wilson International Center for Scholars and Cambridge University Press, 1989), pp. 23-48. Reprinted by permission of Woodrow Wilson International Center for Scholars.

Chapter Six: Adapted from "A Case of the Excluded Middle: Creation Versus Evolution in America," in Robert Bellah and Frederick Greenspahn, eds., *Uncivil Religion: Interreligious Hostility in America* (New York: Crossroad, 1987). Copyright © 1987 by the University of Denver. Reprinted by permission. A shorter version was published as "Creation versus Evolution: No Middle Way," *Nature* 305 (5935, October 13, 1983), 571-74. Copyright © 1983 Macmillan Journals Limited. Reprinted by permission.

Chapter Seven: Adapted from "Understanding J. Gresham Machen," *Princeton Seminary Bulletin* 11/1, new series (February 1990). Delivered as the Frederick Neumann Lecture for 1989 at Princeton Theological Seminary.

*   *   *

I am especially grateful to the Pew Charitable Trusts and to the Divinity School, Duke University, for their ongoing generous support of my work on the topic of the religious and the secular in modern America.

Introduction: Defining Fundamentalism and Evangelicalism

A FUNDAMENTALIST IS AN EVANGELICAL who is angry about something. That seems simple and is fairly accurate. Jerry Falwell has even adopted it as a quick definition of fundamentalism that reporters are likely to quote. A more precise statement of the same point is that an American fundamentalist is an evangelical who is militant in opposition to liberal theology in the churches or to changes in cultural values or mores, such as those associated with "secular humanism." In either the long or the short definitions, fundamentalists are a subtype of evangelicals and militancy is crucial to their outlook. Fundamentalists are not just religious conservatives, they are conservatives who are willing to take a stand and to fight.[1]

This definition would be fairly clear if we knew exactly what an evangelical is. However, our task is made more difficult because neither fundamentalism nor evangelicalism is a clearly defined religious organization with a membership list. Rather, both evangelicalism and fundamentalism are religious *move-*

---

1. Although the term "fundamentalist" was invented in America in 1920 to apply to militant evangelicals, it has in recent years been applied by analogy to any militantly traditionalist religion, such as Islamic fundamentalism.

1

ments. Each of these movements, though only informally organized, is an identifiable set of groups and individuals with some common history and traits. So we may talk about each movement as a whole, as when we say fundamentalists are militant. At the same time, it is just as true that each of these movements is a coalition of submovements, which are sometimes strikingly diverse and do not always get along.

Most of this diversity grows out of the complexity of the evangelical movement, which we must consider briefly in order to see the overall picture. "Evangelical" (from the Greek for "gospel") eventually became the common British and American name for the revival movements that swept back and forth across the English-speaking world and elsewhere during the eighteenth and nineteenth centuries. Central to the evangelical gospel was the proclamation of Christ's saving work through his death on the cross and the necessity of personally trusting him for eternal salvation. In America, the way for the revivals had been prepared in part by the strong Puritan heritage of New England. Nevertheless, the revivalists' emphases on simple biblical preaching in a fervent style that would elicit dramatic conversion experiences set the standards for much of American Protestantism. Since Protestantism was by far the dominant religion in the United States until the mid-nineteenth century, evangelicalism shaped the most characteristic style of American religion.

Being a style as well as a set of Protestant beliefs about the Bible and Christ's saving work, evangelicalism touched virtually all American denominations. These denominations, such as the Methodists, Baptists, Presbyterians, Congregationalists, Disciples of Christ, and others, had much to do with shaping American culture in the nineteenth century. Most major reform movements, such as antislavery or temperance, had a strong evangelical component. Evangelicals had a major voice in American schools and colleges, public as well as private, and had much to do with setting dominant American moral standards.

Especially in its nineteenth-century heyday, then, evangelicalism was a very broad coalition, made up of many sub-groups. Though from differing denominations, these people were united with each other, and with persons from other nations in their zeal to win the world for Christ.

As described in chapter one of this volume, the vast cultural changes of the era from the 1870s to the 1920s created a major crisis within this evangelical coalition. Essentially it split in two. On the one hand were theological liberals who, in order to maintain better credibility in the modern age, were willing to modify some central evangelical doctrines, such as the reliability of the Bible or the necessity of salvation only through the atoning sacrifice of Christ. On the other hand were conservatives who continued to believe the traditionally essential evangelical doctrines. By the 1920s a militant wing of conservatives emerged and took the name fundamentalist. Fundamentalists were ready to fight liberal theology in the churches and changes in the dominant values and beliefs in the culture. By the middle of that decade they had gained wide national prominence. By a few years later, however, their support faded and they disappeared from the headlines.

Since fundamentalism was originally just the name for the militantly conservative wing of the evangelical coalition, fundamentalism was at first almost as broad and complicated a coalition as evangelicalism itself. It included militant conservatives among Baptists, Presbyterians, Methodists, Disciples, Episcopalians, holiness groups, pentecostals, and many other denominations.

After fundamentalism lost its initial national prominence by the 1930s, the term "fundamentalism" began to take on a more limited meaning. Many fundamentalists were leaving the mainline Protestant denominations, essentially those as-sociated with the ecumenical Federal (later National) Council of Churches. Having made this move themselves, fundamen-talists began to make separation from such denominations a test of true faith. The change in terminology was gradual; but by the 1960s "fundamentalist" usually meant separatists and no longer included the many conservatives in mainline de-

3

nominations. Such fundamentalists also stayed separate from two related revivalist movements, the holiness movement and pentecostalism (see chapter one). By this time almost all fundamentalists were Baptists and most were dispensationalists (also see chapter one). The major exception was the Southern Baptist Convention, where a large militantly conservative party was often called "fundamentalist," at least by its opponents.

Fundamentalism then has become a rather specific self-designation. Though outsiders to the movement sometimes use the term broadly to designate any militant conservative, those who call themselves fundamentalists are predominantly separatist Baptist dispensationalists. Jerry Falwell provides a good example. Despite building the Moral Majority as a broader political coalition in the 1980s, in church affairs Falwell remained a separatist Baptist. A notorious instance in 1987 illustrated the tensions between Falwell's role as leader of a coalition and his more narrow church role. When scandal broke around Jim and Tammy Bakker's PTL Ministry, Falwell agreed to step in and take over as a temporary manager. Why he did this is anybody's guess and the arrangement did not last long. One of the most predictable of the many problems, however, was that Falwell's presence caused strong resentment from some PTL constituency. Jim and Tammy were pentecostal; Falwell was a fundamentalist Baptist who in his church condemned pentecostalism.

EVANGELICALISM TODAY

While fundamentalism has become a fairly precise designation for a particular type of Protestant militant, it should be apparent that evangelicalism describes a much more diverse coalition. Roughly speaking, evangelicalism today includes any Christians traditional enough to affirm the basic beliefs of the old nineteenth-century evangelical consensus. The essential evangelical beliefs include (1) the Reformation doctrine of the final authority of the Bible, (2) the real historical character of

God's saving work recorded in Scripture, (3) salvation to eternal life based on the redemptive work of Christ, (4) the importance of evangelism and missions, and (5) the importance of a spiritually transformed life.[2] By this account evangelicalism includes striking diversities: holiness churches, pentecostals, traditionalist Methodists, all sorts of Baptists, Presbyterians, black churches in all these traditions, fundamentalists, pietist groups, Reformed and Lutheran confessionalists, Anabaptists such as Mennonites, Churches of Christ, Christians, and some Episcopalians, to name only some of the most prominent types. In recent decades, opinion surveys that test for evangelical beliefs typically find somewhere around fifty million Americans who fit the definition.[3]

"Evangelicalism," however, does not refer simply to a broad grouping of Christians who happen to believe some of the same doctrines; it can also mean a self-conscious interdenominational movement, with leaders, publications, and institutions with which people from many subgroups identify. Evangelicalism in this sense, which is described in detail in chapter two, refers to what may be called "card-carrying" evangelicals. By contrast, many other persons who would be classified as evangelical in the broad sense of sharing the essential beliefs find their religious identity almost exclusively within their own denomination. This would be true, for instance, of most black Protestants, many Southern Baptists, Churches of Christ, ethnic confessional groups such as Lutheran or Reformed, Mennonites, and many smaller groups. So the test of being a card-carrying evangelical is that

---

2. Lutherans use the term "evangelical" in the broader German sense as roughly the equivalent of "Protestant" or even "Christian," as in the large Evangelical Lutheran Church, organized in 1988. Some neo-orthodox theologians have also used the term in its broad sense of "gospel-believer." The definition offered here, however, reflects the dominant Anglo-American usage.

3. See, for instance, James Davison Hunter, *American Evangelicalism: Conservative Religion and the Quandary of Modernity* (New Brunswick: Rutgers University Press, 1983).

5

of having a fairly strong transdenominational identity, whatever happens to be one's denominational affiliation.

During the 1950s and 1960s the simplest, though very loose, definition of an evangelical in the broad sense was "anyone who likes Billy Graham." Moreover, in the narrow card-carrying sense, most of those who called themselves evangelicals during that period were affiliated with organizations that had some connection with Graham. As chapter two of this volume emphasizes, however, the diverse growth of evangelicalism since the 1960s, especially in its charismatic and pentecostal branches, has expanded the movement as both a broad category and a more specific self-definition. No one leader or set of spokespersons can begin to speak for the whole movement.

Despite this diversity, most of those who would be classed as evangelicals today share considerable common history. Some groups, such as most blacks, some Mennonites, and some immigrant groups, are exceptions with their own more unique heritages. Certainly, though, our understanding of most of the core groups who might *call* themselves evangelical can be enhanced by looking at their common past. All have been touched in some way by the cultural and religious crisis of a century ago that shook American Protestantism to its core. All have been influenced as well by the rift between the earlier broad fundamentalist coalition and liberal mainline Protestantism. All share to some degree the common experience of becoming outsiders to the most sophisticated modern culture. All are part of a recent evangelical resurgence. While some subgroups share these common experiences more directly than do others, there are enough widely overarching themes to ensure that our current understanding can be illuminated by looking at the past.

PART ONE

HISTORICAL OVERVIEW

1. The Protestant Crisis and the Rise of Fundamentalism, 1870–1930

WHEN EVANGELICALISM REIGNED (1865–1890)

A T THE HEIGHT of the Civil War, Northerners often equated the advances of the Union armies with the advances of Christ's kingdom. When they sang, "Mine eyes have seen the glory of the coming of the Lord," their thoughts were not far from the victories of General Sherman or General Grant. While today such equations may seem farfetched, they made sense to those who first sang "The Battle Hymn of the Republic." American Protestants at midcentury frequently had proclaimed that a Christian millennium was not far away. Theirs was an age of great revivals that, if continued, seemed capable of bringing the majority of the citizenry to Christ. National, and even world, reforms would mark this marvelous Christian millennial era. Already American Christianity was identified with the freedoms of democracy. Progress toward other reforms was apparent on numerous fronts. Drinking, sabbath-breaking, prostitution, Romanism, and Freemasonry all were opposed by formidable organizations. Slavery, however, seemed the leading obstacle to America's becoming a fully righteous Christian nation. If it were eliminated, even at the

9

cost of a bloody apocalyptic struggle, little would stand in the way of the advancing kingdom. Surely a golden age was at hand.

The "Gilded Age"

What followed was in fact the "Gilded Age." The era marked by the assassination of two presidents and the impeachment of another, a stolen election, and a reign of rampant political and business corruption and greed, was well named by Mark Twain. A veneer of evangelical Sunday-school piety covered almost everything in the culture, but no longer did the rhetoric of idealism and virtue seem to touch the core of the materialism of the political and business interests. It was a dime-store millennium.

Outwardly Protestantism prospered. Few Protestants doubted that theirs was a "Christian nation." Though religion in America was voluntary, a Protestant version of the medieval ideal of "Christendom" still prevailed. American civilization, said Protestant leaders, was essentially "Christian." Christian principles held the nation together by providing a solid base of morality in the citizenry. Without principles to govern individual and social responsibility, democracy would be impossible and the nation would fall into tyranny and ruin.

Such claims were plausible. American civilization, while never "Christian" in a strict sense, was held together in part by a shared set of values that had a large Protestant component. Children were taught from an early age to play by the rules, and virtually everyone knew of the Ten Commandments, the value of work, and the idea that virtue should be rewarded. During the Gilded Age these principles were still taught not only in the homes but also in the public schools. The most popular grade school textbooks of the era were *McGuffey's Eclectic Readers*. Between 1826 and 1920 an estimated 122 million of these readers were sold. From them generations of America's public school children learned lessons that included "Respect for the Sabbath Rewarded," "The Goodness of God,"

10

"Religion the Only Basis of Society," "The Righteous Never Forsaken," "The Hour of Prayer," "Work," "No Excellence without Labor," "The Character of a Happy Life," "Sowing and Reaping," "My Mother's Bible," and "The Bible the Best of Classics." In the all-important area of a culture where the ideals of one generation are passed to the next, American virtues were presented in an overwhelmingly Protestant framework.

The Evangelical Empire

Protestants' apparent cultural dominance rested on a strong base of the wealthiest and the oldest American families and institutions. Protestants had been the first to settle almost everywhere in the American colonies and so naturally their heirs held most of the positions of power and influence. Leading Americans of the late nineteenth century almost all had Anglo-Saxon, Scottish, or Germanic names—Johnson, Grant, Hayes, Tilden, Garfield, Blaine, Arthur, Harrison, Cleveland, Gould, Fisk, Rockefeller, Morgan, Carnegie, Howells, Clemens, Moody, Beecher, Brooks—reflecting the continuing strength of these predominantly Protestant ethnic groups. It is hardly surprising, then, that the prevailing moral values of the civilization reflected this heritage.

Somewhat more remarkable is that the specifically Christian aspects of this heritage had not eroded more. In Europe during the same era the winds of frankly secular ideologies were blowing strongly, and one might have expected that America, the land of revolutionary liberal political ideals, might by now have adopted a genial democratic humanism, freed from explicitly Christian dogmas and institutions. The fact that America had not in the nineteenth century followed the course set in the eighteenth by leaders like Franklin and Jefferson was due largely to vigorous evangelical enterprise. The United States had not drifted religiously during the nineteenth century. It had been guided, even driven, by resourceful evangelical leaders who effectively channeled the powers of revivals

11

and voluntary religious organizations to counter the forces of purely secular change.

At the heart of the evangelical empire were the great denominations, led by the Methodists, the Baptists, the Presbyterians, the Disciples of Christ, and the Congregationalists, all centers of energetic organization and respectability. Except for the unhealed denominational divisions between North and South, the evangelicalism of these and related groups still presented a united front. Numerous interdenominational organizations—for missions, evangelism, Sunday schools, Bible distribution, moral crusades, social work, and publications—sealed an essential evangelical unity within the context of friendly denominational rivalries. Moreover, steady growth, both in actual numbers and relative to the population, characterized evangelical and other American religious groups during the whole era into the early decades of the twentieth century. Major Protestant groups in fact tripled their membership from 1860 to 1900.

A famous example makes the point. In the 1880s the nation's best-known infidel, Robert Ingersoll, announced that "the churches are dying out all over the land." Charles McCabe of the Methodist Church Extension Society replied by telegram:

> Dear Robert:
>
> All hail the power of Jesus' name—we are building more than one Methodist church for every day in the year, and propose to make it two a day!

The evangelical establishment, as successful as it was in many respects, confronted an unusually severe set of problems. First of all, it faced unprecedented tests intellectually. Skeptics like Robert G. Ingersoll were brandishing with considerable skill a new set of weapons for their views. The publication of Charles Darwin's *Origin of Species* in 1859 had sparked an intellectual crisis for Christians that no educated person could ignore. Darwinism focused the issue on the reliability of the first chapters of Genesis. But the wider issue was whether the Bible could be trusted at all. German higher criticism, questioning the historicity of many biblical accounts, had been developing for more than a generation, so that it was highly sophisticated by the time after the Civil War when it became widely known in America. It would be difficult to overstate the crucial importance of the absolute integrity of the Bible to the nineteenth-century American evangelical's whole way of thinking. When this cornerstone began to be shaken, major adjustments in the evangelical edifice had to be made from top to bottom.

Urbanization and Secularization

The uniquely disconcerting feature of the post–Civil War era was that this staggering intellectual crisis coincided exactly with a social crisis for Protestantism of equally gigantic proportions. American Protestantism had grown up in an era of villages and towns, and so its institutions were adjusted to such settings. In a town, even if many of the people were not actually communicant members of a church, most had family and nominal ties with a denomination so that evangelical beliefs and moral standards enjoyed considerable support from an influential social consensus. In a city such support disappeared. Anonymity, lack of tight Protestant community, and hosts of other attractions eroded church loyalties. Americans, moreover, were moving to the cities in unprecedented numbers. By the beginning of the twentieth century the nation would be approaching the point where most people lived in the cities, whereas only a generation before it had been overwhelmingly rural. As the historian Henry Adams observed in 1905 of his own experience: "the American boy of 1854 stood nearer the year 1 than to the year 1900."

The church crisis associated with massive urbanization was all the more difficult for Protestants because the new industrial workers crowding the cities were not just moving in from the countryside, but were coming largely from abroad. Most of these, moreover, now were coming from Catholic, and increasing from non-English-speaking countries. So while between 1860 and 1900 the major Protestant churches tripled in members (from five million to sixteen million) the Catholic membership quadrupled (from three million to twelve million). Many Protestants saw this steady rise of Catholicism as a major threat to the national welfare. Catholics did not keep the sabbath, they danced, being Europeans most of them drank, and since they were often poor, they were regarded as a threat to the stability and moral health of the nation generally. Nonetheless, there was little that Protestants could do but learn to live with Catholics, however mutually bitter the rivalries might be. The facts of the matter for Protestants were simple. In a nation with a large Catholic (and other non-Protestant) population, they could not simultaneously claim to believe in democracy and also claim that Protestant ideals and values should always rule. This logic, of course, did not prevent widespread anti-Catholic, anti-Jewish, and anti-"foreign" efforts. Nonetheless Protestants, especially in the cities, were faced with the fact that they would have to live with irreversible religious pluralism.

Further compounding the massiveness of the crisis was simply a basic secularization of American culture. The process was more difficult to see since church membership was rising, so this secularization was not taking the most obvious form of simple decline of interest in religious institutions. The opposite seemed true. Yet a steady decline in religious influences was just as certainly well under way. Gradually, various areas of American culture were drifting away from any real connections with religious influences.

Higher education and science reflected this trend most dramatically during the period after the Civil War. In 1850 the vast majority of American colleges had for their presidents evangelical clergymen who ensured a distinctly evangelical and moral flavor in key courses on "moral science," "political economy," or "evidences of Christianity." American science similarly was dominated by evangelical Christians. The chief reason to study nature had been to glory at the marvels of God's design. At midcentury evangelical scientists had confidently proclaimed the scientific confirmations of the Bible. By the end of the century all this seemed almost as distant as the era of the dinosaurs. The best colleges were now "universities" or imitators of universities. Universities, in turn, were based on a German scientific model. Each area, whether it was economics, political science, sociology, psychology, or even history and literary criticism, had become a separate professional discipline. Professional standards no longer were influenced by the Bible, but rather were modeled after the standards of the natural sciences. In the natural sciences themselves, few self-respecting practitioners would publicly reflect on the relation of scientific work to Scripture. Darwinism had seen to that. Instead of science supporting the argument that the design in the universe proved there was a designer, people now talked of "the warfare between science and religion." Within hardly a generation, vast areas of American thought and academic life had been removed from all reference to Protestant or biblical considerations.

In other areas of American life the process of their separation from religious concerns was less dramatic largely because it had been going on for much longer. This was true of economic life and politics, two activities near the heart of the culture. One would have to think back to the early days of the Puritans or the Quakers to appreciate the extent of the change. In any case, by the Gilded Age it was clear that these activities seldom came under real religious review. Moral considerations, with some genuinely Christian roots, could occasionally have an impact, as they did in the Progressive movement after the turn of the century. By and large, however, American politics operated by its own rules, effectively free from internalized moral restraints. So Henry Adams lamented in his novel, *Democracy* (1880). He characterized the nation's leading Washington politician as a person who "talked about virtue and vice as a man who is colour-blind talks about red and

15

green." The business world operated with a similar relationship between Christian and ethical concerns and practical considerations. John D. Rockefeller, Sr., an active Baptist, might say "God gave me my money," even though he gained much of it by shrewd monopolistic practices that drove his competitors out of business. Andrew Carnegie might preach a frankly more secular "Gospel of Wealth." In either case, the religious and moral concerns seemed directed toward justifying what the competitive demands for business success would have dictated anyway.

American Protestants in the late nineteenth century, then, faced a peculiar situation. Externally, they were successful. One could see that from the great stone edifices that were gracing the street corners of cities and towns. Internally, also, they could point to some real spiritual health. Millions of men, women, and young people were profiting from their ministry, growing spiritually, and dedicating their lives toward serving God and their fellows. Enthusiasm for foreign missions, for instance, had never been higher, and the motives for those who made arduous journeys to foreign lands were often self-sacrificial. Many others served their neighbors in quiet ways that were never recorded. And while in many public areas the impact of Protestant Christianity was receding, in countless private ways—especially in family life and the teaching of virtue and responsibility—the influences were strong and positive.

Nonetheless the success was deceptive. Behind it, as has been seen, lurked problems of immense magnitude: formidable intellectual challenges were eroding faith in the Bible, and massive migration to cities and immigration of non-Protestant people produced a secularism that removed much of the nation's life from effective religious influence. The problems were huge, perhaps in human terms insurmountable. Yet the success itself had a tendency to obscure the dimensions of the crises. It also sometimes had the effect of inviting superficial solutions, such as working to preserve Protestant respectability but at the expense of a prophetic Protestant message that would challenge, rather than simply confirm, the value systems that were coming to control American life.

THE STARS

The careers of the most popular religious figures of the era probably are more revealing of the Protestantism of the era than are the histories of the major denominations. Denominations did indeed command loyalties, especially when tied to one's ethnic heritage. But in America the popular belief was strong that the individual was the basic religious unit. Denominational affiliation was ultimately a matter of free choice. As a result, the denominational structures were somewhat weak. If you did not like one church, you could simply leave and go to the one down the street. Accordingly, the strongest religious loyalties of many people were attractive preachers. This trait became particularly apparent after the Civil War when, as in the business world of the same time, this sort of free enterprise system produced great stars who rose to the top in the competition for public acclaim. These traits and the messages of these religious stars are quite revealing, therefore, of popular Protestant opinion.

Henry Ward Beecher

The most famous preacher of the era was Henry Ward Beecher (1813-1887). Beecher was from the first family of nineteenth-century Protestantism. His father, Lyman Beecher, was second in fame only to Charles Finney as a Congregationalist and Presbyterian leader. Several of Lyman's children were illustrious, including Harriet Beecher Stowe, known everywhere as the author of *Uncle Tom's Cabin*. Henry Ward Beecher was almost as well known and was widely regarded as representative of all that was forward-looking in American Protestantism.

For forty years (from 1847 to 1887) Henry was pastor of

the Plymouth (Congregational) Church of Brooklyn, New York. Brooklyn in that day was a thriving middle-class suburb, a prototype of the suburban culture that would characterize twentieth-century America. Beecher's role was to smooth the way in making the religious transition from one era to another. The religious heritage of pious Americans of older Anglo-Saxon stock had been strongly Calvinistic. Henry's father, Lyman, had been known in Boston as "Brimstone Beecher." Now, however, the polite modern temper of suburbia seemed unsuited for the harsher Calvinist doctrines such as total depravity or God's eternal decrees to elect some to salvation and leave others to the endless flames of Hell. Modern thought, especially Darwinism, raised further questions about the basis for traditional beliefs. Beecher, the chief popularizer of the "new theology," reassured his audiences that Christianity progressed with the modern age. One need not worry about the literal accuracy of biblical doctrines. The oaks of civilization, he said, had evolved since biblical times. Should we then "go back and talk about acorns?" The religion of the modern age, moreover, was a matter of the heart rather than a question of strictly orthodox doctrine. Such sentiments appealed to the romantic sensibilities of the time. Christianity, Beecher assured his audiences, had evolved into the highest ethical principles.

The appeal of this message was immense. Sidestepping but not denying many traditional doctrines, Beecher identified Christianity with the highest ideals of respectable middle-class culture. So great was his prestige that his reputation survived a scandal in which in 1874 he was accused of having seduced the wife of one of his parishioners. The jury was out eight days and after fifty-two ballots was unable to agree on a verdict. So Beecher was presumed innocent, perhaps exonerated, and quickly returned to his role as leading American saint. His prestige was demonstrated a few years later when members of the regional congregational association were taking steps to bring heresy charges against his theological doctrines. Beecher simply left the association. The individual had become more influential than the institution.

18

Phillips Brooks

Slightly less colorful, but nearly as much revered, was Beecher's counterpart in Boston, Phillips Brooks (1835-1893). Brooks, like Beecher, could point to Puritan lineage, and as rector of the Trinity Episcopal Church from 1869 to 1893 he helped ease his Boston congregation away from the remaining vestiges of the rigors of the Calvinist heritage. Brooks was an early representative of a line of positive thinkers in American pulpitry. "Believe in yourself," he advised, "and reverence your own human nature; it is the only salvation from brutal vice and every false belief. . . ." His views of human nature were, in fact, just the opposite of those of Calvinism. "The ultimate fact of human life, " he said, "is goodness and not sin." Like every popular American preacher in the modern era, Brooks had a great faith in America itself. "I do not know how a man can be an American," he said in sentiments endlessly reflected by American preachers and their audiences, ". . . and not catch something with regard to God's purpose as to this great land." And, like Beecher, Brooks was a master at integrating modern thought and Christianity into an optimistic, though socially and politically conservative, "American" message.

Josiah Strong

Much as Brooks in "The Law of Growth" used Darwinism to explain a Christianity of self-help and individualism, Josiah Strong (1847-1916) applied Darwinism to suggest new dimensions of Christian American nationalism. Strong was a star of a different sort than Beecher or Brooks. He rose to fame from a book, *Our Country* (1885), which quickly became a best-seller. Strong was a secretary of the Congregational Home Mission Society, and his book was frankly a plea for more vigorous Christian missionary efforts throughout the nation. Perceptive in defining the social dimensions of the American crisis, Strong frankly urged Christianization. "Christianize the immigrant," he declared, "and he will be easily Americanized." The situa-

19

tion was becoming desperate. "Our cities, which are gathering together the most dangerous elements of our civilization, will, in due time, unless Christianized, prove the destruction of our free institutions." Strong's views reflected current social Darwinistic theories about race. He believed that the Anglo-Saxons were proving their superiority by their survival and growing dominance around the world. The superiority of the British and American peoples was seen in their Protestant and democratic principles. The white man, however, had a duty to strengthen other races by sharing with them these ideals, especially Christianity.

Views such as Strong's had a definite effect on American foreign policy. The most famous and striking instance is when during the Spanish-American War (1898) President William McKinley was faced with the question of what to do with the Philippines, recently won from the Spanish. Late one night after kneeling in prayer, he reached the solution: "There was nothing left for us to do but to take them all and to educate the Filipinos and uplift and civilize and Christianize them, and by God's grace do the very best we could by them, as our fellow men for whom Christ also died."

Russell H. Conwell

Baptist Russell H. Conwell (1843-1925), who in Philadelphia built America's largest church, responded to the missionary needs of the day with another version of the gospel of uplift. Conwell, like Josiah Strong, saw the cities as the critical area for home missionary efforts. Not as content as Beecher or Brooks to preach only to those who had arrived socially, the Baptist pastor worked strenuously to make his church responsive also to those who had not yet reached the Protestant middle class. Conwell accordingly made his Baptist Temple into an "institutional church," or a center for social service institutions to serve the neighborhood throughout the week. His complex of institutions offered gymnasiums, athletic programs, reading rooms, day nurseries, educational lectures and cultural activities, a college (eventually Temple University), and the Conwell School of Theology.

While Conwell was a social reformer and philanthropist who responded to the changing needs of the city, his message was that people should help themselves. Conwell was one of the most famous lecturers in America. He delivered his lecture, "Acres of Diamonds," an incredible six thousand times (which would mean an average of 150 repetitions a year for forty years), perhaps the most well-worn discourse in history! Its message was one of success. Specifically, it was the duty of Christians to become rich: you can find acres of diamonds in your own backyard if you only look.

Dwight L. Moody

Dwight L. Moody (1837-1899), the leading professional evangelist of the day, illustrated the American dream of success in his own life. Moody was a Horatio Alger figure. Reared in a small town in New England, he developed a successful shoe business in Chicago but soon turned to evangelism. After some profitable years in local work, he and his singing partner, Ira Sankey, traveled to Great Britain for a modestly conceived preaching tour. The tour in fact became an immense success and lasted from 1873 to 1875. When they returned home Moody and Sankey were national heroes. Through the rest of his career Moody held massive evangelistic campaigns in cities throughout America.

Moody was not a sensationalist evangelist like Charles Finney before him or Billy Sunday in the next generation. Rather, he looked like one of the businessmen of the era and captivated his audiences with a homey and sentimental style of storytelling.

His message was simple. It involved "Three R's": Ruin by Sin, Redemption by Christ, and Regeneration by the Holy Ghost. Saving souls was his preeminent goal. "I look upon this world as a wrecked vessel," he said in his most famous remark. "God has given me a lifeboat and said to me, 'Moody, save all you can.'"

21

This stress on saving souls out of a wrecked world reflected some change in emphasis in popular American evangelism. Many Protestants since the Civil War were losing confidence in social solutions to the world's problems. One sign
of this shift was the increasing popularity of premillennialism,
which emphasized that the world would not be improved until
Jesus personally came again and set up his kingdom on earth.
Moody and all his closest associates preached such doctrines.
Their premillennialism, however, did not lead to complacency.
Rather, it impelled them to more vigorous missionary and
evangelistic efforts ("save all you can"). Moody himself established centers out of which such work radiated. In Chicago he
adopted in 1886 a Bible Institute (later called Moody Bible
Institute) to train laymen for evangelistic efforts. More important at the time were his Northfield Conferences, held near
his Massachusetts home. Out of these grew one of the largest
missionary efforts of the era, the Student Volunteer Movement
founded in 1886. Thousands of students during the subsequent years pledged themselves to lives of missionary work.
The motto of SVM well summarized Moody's own goals: "The
evangelization of the world in this generation."

THE ERA OF CRUSADES (1890-1917)

The motto of the Student Volunteer Movement summarized
well the spirit of much of the American Protestantism of the
day. Not only was it an era of great piety and enthusiasm; it
was also an era of go-getters. To get something done, one had
to approach it with enthusiasm and organization. The sky was
the limit if one organized enthusiasm efficiently. The most
efficient organizations were voluntary ones—people enlisted
and dedicated to a specific cause. So the real cutting edges of
American Protestantism were voluntary organizations and
crusades. By these means vast networks of Protestants from all
major denominations were mobilized for Christian missions
and service.

Dwight Moody's career epitomized this trend. While remaining on the best of terms with denominations, Moody spurned denominational affiliations and built his own evangelistic empire, free from ecclesiastical control. Moody's evangelistic career itself had in fact begun in one of the most important of the earlier parachurch organizations — the Young Men's Christian Association. Imported from England, as were many such evangelical organizations, the YMCA and the YWCA were designed at midcentury as centers for evangelism to young persons moving to the cities. As such they were important components in the evangelical home missionary efforts.

Missions

Missions, whether as evangelism at home or in efforts abroad, were the central Protestant crusades. American Protestants had been active in missions abroad since early in the century, but their enthusiasm burgeoned after 1890. Together with their British counterparts they were leading an advance of Christian missions so great that historian Kenneth Scott Latourette has called the period from 1815 to 1914 "the great century" of Christian missions. Certainly in America the period from 1890 to World War I was the golden age of Protestant missions.

Efforts to mobilize at home were equally ambitious. Prior to the Civil War there had been an "empire" of evangelical agencies for home and foreign missions, Sunday schools, Bible and tract distribution, benevolence, and reform. In the postwar era these "voluntary societies," often cooperating with denominational agencies, continued to provide the leading edge in organizing spiritual impulses.

The growth of the Sunday-school movement is a good example. For a generation the American Sunday School Union, based on a British agency, had been evangelizing children throughout the nation. With the growth of the cities after the Civil War Sunday schools appeared as most important means for reaching the unchurched. Often families could be reached through their children. Enterprising leaders accordingly revitalized the Sunday-school movement by introducing new organizations and techniques. Under the leadership of the Baptist B. F. Jacobs, "decision days" and "rally days" were organized. Teachers were brought together in regular county conventions, and a "uniform lesson" plan was devised so that members of various denominations could meet together to prepare the next week's lesson. Young people and adults were also mobilized through Sunday-school classes so that the whole Protestant community might be turned into an agency for evangelism. "Each one win one" became the motto for many Baraca (for men) and Philathea (for women) classes by the turn of the century, and by 1913 these nationally organized classes were involving a total of nearly one million members from thirty-two denominations and had spawned many imitators. Sunday schools sometimes even overshadowed the local congregation, and the Sunday-school superintendent might be nearly as important a figure as the minister.

A similar case is the growth of the Christian Endeavor Society. Francis E. Clark, a Congregationalist minister, founded this organization in Maine in 1881 "to promote earnest Christian life" and to provide training for Christian service. Typically, Christian Endeavor groups held weekly devotional meetings and monthly meetings for special consecration. "Trusting in the Lord Jesus Christ for strength," read the simple pledge, "I promise Him I will strive to do whatever He would have me do." Clark's organization grew so rapidly among young people that by 1885 he could found an international organization, claiming 3.5 million members by 1910, with perhaps two-thirds of these in the United States and Canada. Such enterprises had the important side effect of uniting Protestants from almost every denomination.

In this context the more famous crusades of the era should be viewed. Of these the most successful was the temperance movement, which attempted to ban the use of alcoholic beverages. This movement, as many others, had substantial roots from earlier in the nineteenth century but was effectively revived and efficiently organized during the new age of crusading Protestantism. Temperance was an issue on which liberals and conservatives could thoroughly agree, and one of the few issues on which Protestants could make common cause with some Catholic leaders.

By contrast, the least successful of the major campaigns was the crusade for sabbath observance. The Puritan sabbath, in which the Lord's Day was strictly observed for worship rather than work or play, was one of the chief symbols of Protestant civilization in America. European immigrants, both from some Protestant groups who were not Sabbatarian and especially from Catholic countries, threatened this custom. Their "continental sabbath" was more like a holiday. Secularization favored the continental trend as well, as did some Protestant reaction to overly strict sabbath-keeping. Many Protestants fought staunchly, however, to enforce their sabbath customs by legislation, attempting to ban commercial enterprises, industries, and places of amusement from operating on the sabbath. Particularly notorious were efforts to close the Centennial Exposition of Philadelphia on Sundays in 1876 and the Columbian Exposition in Chicago in 1893. In the latter instance, Sabbatarian efforts were thoroughly defeated. Throughout the era, however, businesses and industries in most areas remained closed on Sunday.

Both the temperance campaigns and Sabbatarianism were viewed among their proponents as not only questions of personal morality but also important social reforms. Alcoholic consumption was often viewed as a "drug" problem in the cities in much the same way as narcotic drugs have been more recently. Urban poverty often seemed related to squandering money, time, and energy on alcohol. Sabbatarianism was viewed in a similar light. Before effective labor unions, when industrialists often required their employees to work sixty-hour weeks or even more, enforced sabbath rest was an important piece of labor legislation. Paradoxically, Protestant zeal had not carried over to other labor reforms so that a Sabbatarianism that banned recreation as well as work on Sunday held only slim attractions for those who had to work almost every waking hour for six days a week.

Women as Reformers

The evangelical activism and reforms of this era were closely connected with changing roles of women. These changes pointed in a number of directions. One of the strongest impulses among the Protestants who dominated the culture was the exaltation of women's role in the home. Balancing some of the individualism and competitive business mentality of the day was the belief that the society was only as strong as its most basic institutions, the home and the church. While churches typically allowed only males to be ordained, in the home women were expected to be moral and spiritual leaders. This role was seen as having a major function as well, since women were regarded as the chief guardians of society's highest values. Countless men and women testified to having learned such values on their mother's knee.

A similar view of women's moral and spiritual superiority fostered the gradual expansion of their public roles as well. Women constituted more than half of church members and the churches were one of the first public forums in which they were permitted to organize. During this era the vast majority of women's organizations were church societies. In these women sought to extend their roles as promoters of religion and virtue. During this time when the missionary movement reached its peak, women were the mainstays of local support. Moreover, many women served as missionaries, not only as coworkers with their husbands, but often also as single women who were allowed in foreign settings greater leadership roles than church order typically permitted in America.

Women's church organization promoted a host of charitable and reform efforts as well, some of which moved them toward the political arena. The most conspicuous of these was the temperance movement, in which women's contributions were central. Playing a major part in organizing church women for this campaign was the Women's Christian Temperance Union, headed by Frances Willard (1839-1898) from 1874 to 1898. Willard was an ardent Methodist who was convinced that

Christians' moral force should combat the leading drug problem of the day.

Zeal for such causes strengthened demands to allow women the vote. Frances Willard and many other activist women saw women's suffrage and social reform going hand in hand. Typically they argued that if women were morally and spiritually superior, society would gain dramatically if they were allowed the vote.

Within the Protestant churches there were parallel demands for opening church offices to women. In the second half of the nineteenth century a few women were ordained to the ministry, but such reforms were largely outside the mainstream of American Protestantism. Some of the more liberal New England churches ordained women; but the most striking gains came in some of the new holiness churches, which allowed women preaching and ordination as signs of a new age of the outpouring of the Holy Spirit. In most mainstream Protestant churches secondary church offices were opened to women by the 1920s and ordination to the ministry allowed by the 1950s. Many conservative Protestants, however, resisted such innovations.

Social Involvement and Retraction

As American Protestants moved from the nineteenth to the twentieth century they were facing a broad range of new social problems that could divide them over what direction their moral zeal should lead them. It was one thing to believe that Christians should organize for a better society; it was another to know exactly what would make a society better.

The rise of urban poverty, for instance, precipitated a crisis in the Protestant conscience. During the latter decades of the nineteenth century the prevailing convictions about self-help and laissez-faire economics, together with considerable distrust or dislike of the new American working classes and their unions, stood in the way of dealing with the problems at their roots. So when one reads from the prominent church paper *The Congregationalist* in 1886 that in response to labor riots in Chicago "a Gatling gun or two, swiftling brought into position and well served, offers, on the whole, the most merciful as well as effectual remedy," it might appear that the quality of Protestant mercy is a bit strained. *The Congregationalist's* sentiments, however, were not unusual, given the assumptions and social position of most Protestants of the day. Nevertheless, the new problems of the poverty of the teeming cities were too intense, and the American Protestant conscience too tender, for such callous solutions to prevail everywhere. Those Protestant leaders who knew most about the real conditions of the poor during this era often were the evangelists who sought to convert the urban poor. Such work led evangelists to slums and tenements and convinced many of them of the urgency of supplementing preaching with simple Christian charity, such as by providing the poor with ice in the summer and coal in the winter. Groups with strong evangelistic emphases, especially holiness groups such as the Salvation Army but including also some of the leading evangelistic associates of Dwight L. Moody, led in these efforts. The rescue mission movement, serving the down-and-out with food, lodging, and the gospel, provided one of the important new institutions of the era.

Gradually, other Protestants awakened to the enormity of the new social problems facing urban America and began to assume responsibility. In part this was due to work of effective reformers such as that of the Danish immigrant Jacob Riis, whose *How the Other Half Lives* (1890) shocked Victorian sensibilities with its exposure of slum conditions in New York City. More importantly, the political mood of the nation was beginning to shift. During the Gilded Age, conservatism on social issues had prevailed. By 1890, however, winds of change were blowing. The Populist movement, primarily a farmers' movement in the South and the western Midwest, included radical proposals for national social reform. By 1896 Populism had become such a potent political force that it virtually captured the Democratic party with the nomination of the eloquent Christian spokesman for the people, William Jennings Bryan. Another ardent Christian, William McKinley, representing more conservative political assumptions, was elected, but the spirit of reform was in the air. After the death of McKinley in 1901 and the ascendency of Theodore Roosevelt, reformist "progressive" views came to prevail even in the middle classes. Through the election of 1916 every major presidential candidate considered himself "progressive."

This political setting fostered a new wave of social concern in the churches and new types of proposals for social reform. "Social service," concerned with voluntary acts of charity, increased, but new progressive suggestions from Christians for more comprehensively reforming the social and economic order became especially prominent. These progressive proposals came to be known collectively as "the social gospel." Social gospel proponents explicitly rejected the individualism and laissez-faire economics that had prevailed in the Gilded Age and insisted rather that the government take an active part in alleviating the harshest effects of an unrestrained free enterprise system. Their reform proposals were essentially identical with those of the "progressive" politics of the same era. Social gospel advocates tended to make these social concerns central to their understanding of the gospel. While not necessarily denying the value of the traditional evangelical approach of starting with evangelism, social gospel spokesmen subordinated such themes, often suggesting that stress on evangelism had made American evangelicalism too otherworldly (concerned about getting people to heaven) and individualistic (concerned with personal purity more than with the welfare of one's neighbor). Such themes fit well with the emerging liberal theology of the day, which was optimistic about human nature, ethical in emphasis, and hopeful about establishing the principles of the kingdom in the twentieth century. So while some more traditional evangelistically minded evangelicals, such as William Jennings Bryan, might be progressive politically, the social gospel itself came generally to involve an association of progressive politics with liberal and nonevangelistic theology.

This association of progressive politics with liberal theology came at the same time as a deep crisis was brewing over theological issues. The result of this conjunction of theological and social crises was that twentieth-century American Protestantism began to split into two major parties, not only between conservatives and liberals in theology but correspondingly between conservatives and progressives politically. Conservative theology began to be associated with conservative politics and liberal theology with progressive politics. This development, which was gradual, has sometimes been called "the great reversal" in American evangelicalism. Until this time in American history considerable numbers of revivalist evangelicals had always been in the forefront of social and political reform efforts (antislavery, for instance), even though many other evangelicals had been socially conservative. In the twentieth century, however, evangelical participation in progressive reforms, except in some of the older crusades such as for prohibition, dwindled sharply. As theological liberals spoke more and more about the social implications of the gospel, revivalist evangelicals spoke of them correspondingly less.

This division over both the theological and the social issues was only beginning to become apparent in the first two decades of the century. The crusading spirit and a zeal for Protestant unity based on action still prevailed. Despite the deep tensions, said one survivor of the era, "the ten or fifteen years before the war were, controversially, a kind of Truce of God." Nowhere was this more manifest than in the emergence in 1908 of the Federal Council of Churches. This organization for cooperative action among the Protestant denominations embodied many of the same impulses that were uniting Protestants in Christian Endeavor, the Sunday schools, and prohibition campaigns. At this point the social questions were not yet so clearly divisive as to prevent the new ecumenical agency from concentrating first on social issues. These, in fact, were first on its agenda when the new cooperative body met in 1908.

Such vigorous social emphases brought criticism from conservatives, who said that the ecumenical body was losing sight of the central goal of the gospel, of winning souls to Christ. In response, the Federal Council in 1912 balanced its commission on social service by adding a commission on evangelism. The same year saw the culmination of one of the last great united crusades of the era, the Men and Religion Forward Movement. This huge effort attempted to mobilize men and boys for both social service and soul-winning. The effort seemed too much planned, and did not live up to expectations.

A deeper problem was developing, however. Evangelicals who emphasized revivalism and those who emphasized social reform were coming more and more to comprise two parties. This was apparent in another incident in 1912. Billy Sunday, who was just rising to fame as the latest of America's leading evangelists, conducted a revival campaign in Columbus, Ohio. After the campaign Washington Gladden, a Congregationalist pastor in Columbus and one of the leading spokesmen for the social gospel, bitterly criticized Sunday's sensationalist techniques and his gospel of soul-saving. A heated debate developed in the religious press. Sunday, while not condemning social service, charged that the recent emphases were "trying to make a religion out of social service with Jesus Christ left out." He claimed that this was the reason for the failure of the Men and Religion Forward Movement. "We've had enough," he said, "of this godless social service nonsense."

Beneath such accusations were more serious problems that could not be ignored much longer. Activism and good will had kept a semblance of unity within the dominant Protestant community. Divisive theological and intellectual issues were considered best kept away from public attention, and indeed most of the church-going public was not aware of how deep the rift had become. Success and progress still seemed the dominant mood, underlined by much rhetoric about unity, together with activism, and by beating the drums for the latest crusade. Eventually, however, American Protestantism would have to pay the price of sidestepping the hard theological questions. In fact, there were controversies simmering that were too deep to ignore. To understand these requires a closer look at some of the new trends of the day.

NEW DEPARTURES AND CONSERVATIVE RESPONSES (1865-1917)

Beneath the surface unity within middle-class white Protestantism some extremely deep rifts were developing. Like the tremors that presage the eruptions of a volcano, the preliminary manifestations were not entirely indicative of the convulsions that were heating up beneath. So the prevailing mood of Protestants in the era from the Civil War to World War I was one of prosperity, progress, and confidence. The truth of the matter was, however, that vastly different understandings of the gospel were developing. Ultimately these differences were so great as to precipitate what historian Sydney Ahlstrom describes as "the most fundamental controversy to wrack the churches since the Reformation."

Liberalism and Modernism

Perhaps the most important point for understanding theological liberalism or modernism (the terms often are used interchangeably) is that it was a movement designed to save Protestantism. As has been seen, the generations of Protestants that came of age between 1865 and 1917 were faced with the most profound challenges to their faith. Darwinism and higher criticism were challenging the authority of the Bible and the new historical, sociological, and Freudian psychological ways of thinking were revolutionizing thought at almost every level. Immense social changes plus rapid secularization, especially in science and higher education, were eroding Protestantism's practical dominance.

In personal terms, this meant that many people brought up to accept unquestioningly the complete authority of the

Bible and the sure truths of evangelical teaching found themselves living in a world where such beliefs no longer were considered intellectually acceptable. Such was typical of the personal histories of the leaders of the liberal movement. Brought up in moderately well-to-do evangelical homes, they formed close attachments to the Christian faith, although usually they did not have a dramatic conversion experience. When they reached the universities, however, they were confronted with a most difficult choice. They could hang on to evangelicalism at the cost of sacrificing the current standards for intellectual respectability. If they were going to retain such intellectual respectability, it seemed they must either abandon Christianity or modify it to meet the standards of the day. For many the latter choice seemed the only live option. Many church-going people must have shared these liberal sentiments. By the first decades of the century, liberalism, or modernism as it was coming to be called, was well entrenched in almost all of the leading theological seminaries. Probably more than half of Protestant publications leaned toward modernism, and liberals occupied perhaps one-third of the nation's pulpits.

A movement of this proportion and which stressed freedom from tradition (hence the term "liberalism") and adjustment to the modern world (hence "modernism") inevitably encompassed wide variety. Nonetheless, a good picture of the outlook can be gained by considering three of its most typical strategies for saving the faith in the face of the modern intellectual onslaught.

Deifying Historical Process

The first method of responding to the intellectual challenges was for liberals typically to deify historical process. Simply put, this meant that God revealed himself in history and was incarnate in the development of humanity. Christ, who stood at the center of liberal theology and at the center of history, embodied this close relationship between the divine and the historical. The kingdom of Christ was the continuing manifestation of the power of God to change human relationships. The Bible was a record of the religious experience of an ancient people. It was not an encyclopedia of dogma but rather an ancient model of religious experience. Today this model should not be followed slavishly, but its best principles developed as science and modern civilization advance the understanding of God's reconciling actions. The progress of humanity, then, especially in the moral sphere, is identified with the progress of Christ's kingdom.

One of the beauties of this reinterpretation of Christian tradition for the turn-of-the-century church member was that this version of Christianity was immune from the ravages of modern historical and scientific criticism. For that generation, Darwinism provided the standard for thinking about almost everything. Just as Darwin explained biological development through natural processes, so history and society were interpreted in much the same way. The social sciences and new scientific history claimed that human religions were products of social evolution. They were the natural developments in the efforts of the race to adjust to a threatening environment. The Bible, accordingly, was regarded just as any other religious book, the product of the experiences of the Hebrew people. The new Christian liberalism, however, had a striking answer to this challenge. The history of people's religious experiences is just God's way of working. The Bible need not be proven historically or scientifically accurate to be regarded as a faithful rendering of the religious perceptions of the Hebrew people. In their history, however much it might be mixed with human elements, one finds a people who understood God's working with humanity in a unique way. A person can benefit much from this example, even without following it slavishly. Scientific history and biblical criticism were not a threat to such a faith.

Stressing the Ethical

Closely related was a second emphasis of liberalism or modernism that kept it safe from attack. The key test of Christianity was life, not doctrine. Christianity could be saved by stressing the ethical. This, said the liberals, was the heart of Jesus' teaching. Calvinism and other traditional theologies had stressed too much the judicial elements of God's relationship to humanity. Jesus, by contrast, had emphasized the fatherhood of God and the brotherhood of mankind. Whatever else might fall before the withering blasts of criticism, the ethics of Jesus would survive.

In practical terms, such ethical emphases appeared in several varieties. Most liberals stressed Christian education, as in Sunday schools, where moral lessons predominated. This emphasis was consistent with the personal experiences of many liberals who had grown gradually to love the faith through Christian nurture, rather than through a radical conversion experience. Among some of the early liberals, such as Henry Ward Beecher or Phillips Brooks, the content of their ethics often reflected the individualism of the day. In the progressive era, however, liberal leaders such as Washington Gladden and Walter Rauschenbusch rediscovered and developed the social message of the faith. At the popular level, such social concerns were well represented by Charles M. Sheldon's book, *In His Steps* (1896), a moving story of how a congregation was awakened by taking seriously the question, "What would Jesus do?" During the next decades Sheldon's book sold millions of copies, which was no small indication of the power of the Christian ethical challenge to Americans of that day.

The Centrality of the Religious Feelings

The third element widespread in the liberal defense of Christianity was the conviction that religious feelings were central to Christianity. Following the German theologian Friedrich Schleiermacher (1768-1834), liberals held that the basis of religion is the sense of absolute dependence. As with the stress on ethics, religious feelings could readily be contrasted to the religion of reason, dogma, or the literal interpretations of the Bible. Science and historical criticism, moreover, could not touch the intuition of the heart "which reason does not know." Appealing to the romantic and idealistic sentiments of the day, liberal

Christians could let science reign freely in its own domain, but insist on a realm of religious truth that science could not reach.

Conservative Reactions

Though liberals and modernists were sheltering important aspects of their Christian heritage from the challenges of modern thought, they were simultaneously acquiring considerable opposition on their other flank from conservatives who saw their accommodations to modernity as a sell-out. At first, especially during the 1870s and 1880s, the controversies centered on Darwinism. Darwin's theory of evolution by natural selection hit particularly hard at evangelical Protestantism since it undermined the current defenses of the faith at two critical points. First, by implication it questioned the accuracy of the Bible, which had been the most important exhibit in demonstrations of "evidences" for Christianity. Second, Darwinism totally reversed the perceptions of the relation of science to the Christian faith. In the mid-nineteenth century American Christian apologists rested their case heavily on the argument from design. The scientific revolution of the past two centuries, they said, had uncovered some of the marvels of God's intricate and awesome design of the universe. It was inconsistent rationally to believe, they argued, that so complex and orderly a system could lack an intelligent designer. Darwinism, however, posited just the opposite. The apparent design in the universe was best explained by chance. With no prevision of the course of the universe, the species developed their intricate and marvelous structures simply because of the necessities of survival in a brutal universe. The order and apparent design, many scientists now claimed, could be well explained with no reference to God.

As discussed in detail in later chapters of this volume, Protestant reactions to Darwinism varied considerably. If Darwinism had to do simply with biological development, the processes it posited could be subsumed under God's providence. Christians could say, as the popular John Fiske put it, "Evolution is God's way of doing things." Liberal and moderate

36

Protestants took this view. So did some conservatives who usually rejected, however, the purely evolutionary origins of humans as incompatible with Genesis. Other conservatives rejected all biological evolution as contrary to literal readings of Scripture, also because many evolutionists, including Darwin himself, used their claims about biology to support a worldview in which God was excluded. Charles Hodge of Princeton Theological Seminary, for instance, answered the question of his book *What is Darwinism?* (1874) with "it is atheism."

Since even conservative opinions varied, however, views on Darwinism were seldom used as tests of the faith among mainstream Protestants in the late nineteenth century. The major exception was in the South, which after its defeat in the Civil War remained predominantly committed to the conservative Protestantism of the prewar era and suspicious of all innovations.

Whether in South or North, the larger issue was the truth of the Bible. The authority for their whole belief system seemed to rest on this foundation. If the Bible were not true, then on what did Protestantism, the religion of *scriptura sola*, rest? And what if there were scientific and historical errors in Scripture? Would not such flaws call into question other biblical claims? With both Darwinists and highly sophisticated higher critics suggesting that there were serious errors in Scripture, many of the faithful of the turn-of-the-century generation had to be deeply disturbed.

As in the case of Darwinism, conservative Protestants themselves divided over these persistent questions. Some would make virtually no concessions to the new historical analysis of the Bible. The most articulate of these conservative spokespersons were the theologians at the conservative Presbyterian theological seminary in Princeton. Carefully they defined what they took to be the church's traditional stance regarding the Bible. The text as originally inspired by the Holy Spirit, they insisted, was "absolutely errorless." This doctrine of "inerrancy," as it came to be known, was no invention of the late nineteenth century. Many Christians in the past had said or assumed much the same thing. But the fact that now some

37

conservative Protestants were making biblical inerrancy a central doctrine, even sometimes virtually a test of faith, signaled the degree to which the new scientific and historical threats to the Bible were forcing everyone to shore up whatever he or she considered the most critical line of defense.

The rise to prominence of the issues of inerrancy and the Bible's historical accuracy sparked considerable debate. The most spectacular case was that of Prof. Charles A. Briggs (1841-1913) of Union Theological Seminary in New York, a Presbyterian institution. In an inaugural address in 1891, Briggs directly attacked the doctrine of "inerrancy" as articulated by Princeton theologians Archibald Alexander Hodge (1823-1886) and Benjamin Breckinridge Warfield (1851-1921). Although Briggs was a traditionalist in most of his theology, he insisted that Christians ought to face up to the fact that the Bible contained numerous incidental errors not central to its teaching. For this Briggs was brought to trial in the Presbyterian church and suspended from the ministry. The result, however, was that both he and his seminary left the Presbyterian church.

Between 1878 and 1906 almost every major Protestant denomination experienced at least one heresy trial, usually of a seminary professor. As in the Briggs case, however, the conservative efforts seemed to do little to retard the liberal trends. By the early 1900s many Protestant seminaries in the North were controlled by liberals. The (Baptist) Divinity School of the University of Chicago, for instance, had been transformed by this time from an outpost for moderately conservative Baptist evangelicalism to one of the world's leading centers for liberal theology.

The contests between liberals and conservatives, however, did not directly touch most ordinary American Protestants. In 1905 an astute Baptist observer estimated that this moderate conservative party constituted "still the vast majority" of Baptists throughout the nation. Probably ninety-five percent of Baptists, he thought, were not "conscious of any important change in theology or departure from the old Baptist orthodoxy." Even the leadership of Baptist conservatives often declined to take

hard lines. President Augustus H. Strong (1836-1921) of Roch-
ester Theological Seminary, for example, though unquestion-
ably a conservative, explicitly repudiated in his widely used
Systematic Theology the dogma of the inerrancy of Scripture. The
main lines of a conservative defense of Christianity, Strong maintained, should be personal religious experience and practical
morality. President Edgar Young Mullins (1860-1928) of the
Southern Baptist Theological Seminary in Louisville, though an
opponent of liberalism, took his stand on this same experiential
and practical line of defense. Probably for most American Protestants in the pews, especially in the two largest denominations,
the Methodists and the Baptists, such assurances were sufficient
against the rumors of intellectual assault.

Conservative Innovations

Liberals and modernists were not the only Protestants of the
era who met the challenges of the day with substantial innovations. Three other important movements, all essentially conservative on most points of theology and all active in revivalism,
offered new directions for Protestant renewal.

Dispensational Premillennialism

Dispensationalism, or dispensational premillennialism, was the
fruit of renewed interest in the detail of biblical prophecy which
developed after the Civil War. Rejecting the prevailing postmillennialism which taught that Christ's kingdom would grow
out of the spiritual and moral progress of this age, dispensational premillennialists said that the churches and the culture
were declining and that Christians would see Christ's kingdom
only after he personally returned to rule in Jerusalem. They
thus offered a plausible explanation of the difficulties the
church was facing. These failings had been predicted in biblical
prophecy. "Christendom," or "Christian civilization," had always been an illusory ideal. Now that was being made apparent
by the secularization of the culture and the apostasy (liberalism)

within the churches themselves. Yet the Bible also provided firm hope for the coming of the kingdom.

One of the distinctives of dispensationalism was that it posited that the Bible explained all historical change through a pattern of seven dispensations or eras. In each of these dispensations God tested humanity through a different plan of salvation. Humans failed each test, and each era ended in a catastrophic divine judgment. The first dispensation ended with the human Fall into sin and explusion from Eden, the second ended with the Flood, the third with the Tower of Babel, and so forth. We live in the sixth era, or church age, also heading toward catastrophe and divine intervention. Finally, after a tumultuous seven years of wars and calamities, Jesus will establish a literal kingdom in Jerusalem and reign for a thousand years.

Dispensationalists emphasize that their views are based on literal readings of Scripture, especially of biblical prophecies. For instance, they predicted the literal return of the Jews to Israel, as the Bible indicates. Because of their emphasis on literal interpretations of prophecies, dispensationalists have been one of the groups most insistent on making the inerrancy of Scripture a test of true faith.

This new form of premillennial teaching, imported from England, first spread in America through prophecy conferences where the Bible was studied intently. Summer conferences, a newly popular form of vacation in the age of trains, were particularly effective. Most importantly, Dwight L. Moody had sympathies with the broad outlines of dispensationalism and had as his closest lieutenants dispensationalist leaders such as Reuben A. Torrey (1856-1928), James M. Gray (1851-1925), C. I. Scofield (1843-1921), William J. Erdman (1833-1923), A. C. Dixon (1854-1925), and A. J. Gordon (1836-1895). These men were activist evangelists who promoted a host of Bible conferences and other missionary and evangelistic efforts. They also gave the dispensationalist movement institutional permanence by assuming leadership of the new Bible institutes such as the Moody Bible Institute (1886), the Bible Institute of Los Angeles (1907), and the Philadelphia College of the Bible (1914). The network of related institutes that soon sprang up became the nucleus for much of the important fundamentalist movement of the twentieth century. Dispensationalist leaders, in fact, actively organized this antimodernist effort. Notably, they oversaw the publication between 1910 and 1915 of the widely distributed twelve-volume paperback series, *The Fundamentals*. This conservative "Testimony to the Truth," financed by Lyman and Milton Stewart, included writings from a considerable variety of antimodernist spokespersons, including many nondispensationalists such as the Princeton theologians and moderates such as E. Y. Mullins.

Dispensationalism itself was strikingly antimodernist. In many respects it looked like the mirror image of modernism. Modernism was optimistic about modern culture; dispensationalism was pessimistic. Most importantly, each centered around an interpretation of the relation of the Bible to history. Modernism interpreted the Bible through the lens of human history. Dispensationalists interpreted history exclusively through the lens of Scripture. Where modernism stressed the naturalistic, seeing social forces as being crucial to understanding religion, dispensationalists accentuated the supernatural, making divine intervention the direct solution to the modern problem of explaining historical change.

The Holiness Movement

A second major innovative evangelical movement—the holiness movement—may be understood as a mirror image of another modernist theme—the stress on morality. When liberals emphasized the ethical, they typically spoke of the natural tendencies to good in all people. Christianity could cultivate these tendencies and bring them to fruition. The parallel holiness movement also accentuated the ethical, but with the opposite emphasis. The supernatural work of the Holy Spirit was essential to overcome natural tendencies. Moreover, whereas the liberals spoke of gradual cultivation or of Christian education, the advocates of holiness maintained that nothing less than a dramatic work of the Holy Spirit could cleanse the heart

41

of sin. So holiness teachers were distinguished from most other revivalist evangelicals by insisting not only on a dramatic conversion experience but also a definite "second blessing" in which the work of the Spirit freed one from sin's power.

The holiness movement was actually a variety of movements growing out of the teachings of John Wesley. By the mid-nineteenth century holiness teachings were thriving in many different forms, and often went beyond the bounds of Methodism itself. By the second half of the century such teachings were leading to the formation of new denominations. Stressing ethical duty, holiness groups usually were concerned not only with personal purity but also with responsibilities toward the poor. In the latter half of the century, holiness organizations, of which the best known is the Salvation Army, were leaders in Protestant care for the poor and evangelism to the outcasts.

Holiness groups, often separating from the larger and more respectable denominations, and often winning converts from less established people in the immigrant and working classes, tended to have a more modest socioeconomic base than did older groups like Episcopalians, Congregationalists, Presbyterians, and even Baptists and Methodists. This correlation illustrates a general point in modern church life: the more well-to-do a group, the less demanding its requirements for sanctification. Liberal Protestants, as a group, were better off socially than any other body of Protestants. For them virtue was found in the best developments of modern civilization and in their own lives. Traditional denominationalists stood somewhere in the middle, having more ambivalent attitudes toward how much of the world had to be renounced in order properly to live the Christian life. Near the far end of the spectrum were the holiness groups, speaking of much radical separation from worldliness but having, in a material sense, less of the world to renounce.

Pentecostalism

Pentecostalism, which after 1900, developed first in some holiness groups, was even more radical in its teachings and even more prone to attract the socially disinherited. It was for a time, in fact, the only portion of Protestantism to be integrated racially. Again, a contrast with liberalism is helpful. One of the liberal strategies was to emphasize religious experience as an unassailable authentication of Christianity. In a sense, the Pentecostals emphasized the same thing. As in the other cases, however, theirs was a mirror image of the liberal view. Pentecostals accentuated the supernatural just at the point where the liberals stressed the divine elements in the natural. So while modernists might speak of a gentle "religion of the heart" Pentecostals insisted that true heart religion be evidenced by unmistakable signs of the Spirit's radical transforming power, especially the pentecostal signs of faith healing and speaking in tongues.

Faith healing and speaking in tongues were parts of a strong impulse within Pentecostalism to restore the practices of the New Testament church. Pentecostals expected believers not only to have a conversion experience but also to experience a dramatic outpouring of the Holy Spirit and to live a life of holiness. Adopting dispensationalism, they taught that Jesus might return at any moment. All these doctrines, they insisted, were essential to the "full gospel."

Pentecostal growth was sparked especially by the Azusa Street Revivals in Los Angeles beginning in 1906, led by black evangelist William J. Seymour. During the next decade the movement spread into dozens of small denominations, separating into black and white. A number of these were called the Church of God. The largest single denomination was the Assemblies of God, formed in 1914. All of these remained small and relatively poor until the later half of the twentieth century when their missionary efforts burgeoned into a major world movement.

These three new evangelical movements—dispensationalism, holiness, and pentecostalism—were each innovative in its own way; yet they had in common a distinctly antiliberal stress on dramatic intervention of the supernatural. The three, accordingly, have many similarities, and, in fact, there were many interconnections among them. Moody's lieutenant, Reuben A. Torrey, for instance, is revered in all three traditions, although he himself did not agree with the pentecostal demands for visible signs of the Holy Spirit's work. Inevitably, these connections led to controversies and many divisions, resulting in a wide variety of emphases within the three movements. The three, however, united at least in their common opposition to modernism, had much to do with shaping twentieth-century American evangelicalism.

Immigrant Traditionalism

While the mainstream of American Protestantism was fragmenting into many groups, the situation was complicated even more by continued immigration. Vast numbers of the new immigrants were Catholic and sizable groups were Jewish or Eastern Orthodox—all leading to a sense that traditional Protestantism could no longer shape an American public consensus the way it once had. One impulse shaping liberal Protestantism, in fact, was that of a dominant social group hoping to keep its customary control. In increasingly pluralistic America such control was much easier to maintain if Protestant religion was defined in terms of high moral ideals with which few were likely to disagree.

Recent Protestant immigrants, most of whom were northern European—German, Scandinavian, or Dutch—could relatively easily be absorbed into the Protestant mainstream, if they so desired. In the short run, however, many were eager to preserve their ethnic religious heritages. Often they shared theological beliefs with conservative American Protestants, but distrusted the enthusiastic evangelical style of their new neighbors. Especially those ethnically Protestant communities that moved into the farmlands of the Midwest preserved traditional theological outlooks shaped by the standards of the Reformation. After several generations their styles of Christianity inevitably became more like their American counterparts, either evangelical or more liberal, but such processes were often slow.

44

Most such immigrants were Lutheran. Numbering less than a half million in 1870, Lutheranism in America reached well over two million by 1910 and had become the fourth largest religious grouping, behind Catholics, Methodists, and Baptists. Lutheranism at this time, however, was more a grouping than a group. The number of separate Lutheran denominations was well into the dozens and constantly changing through divisions or mergers. Lutherans had almost as much diversity as Catholics, but none of the necessity of working together. They resolved their differences in the meantime largely by remaining apart. This diversity had a number of important sources—degrees of Americanization (some synods used English, for instance, while most did not), ethnic differences (as among Germans, Danes, Swedes, and Norwegians), and geographical separation. Despite these differences, most of the Lutherans manifested a deep commitment to the Augsburg Confession, and many preserved their identity through separate school systems. Notable in these respects was the conservative Missouri Synod. As in American churches generally, World War I brought a sense of unity. Accordingly, it brought a large number of Lutheran mergers. The war with Germany also put large pressures on the churches to Americanize and to abandon the German language.

Reformed churches with northern European heritages, such as the Dutch Reformed and the German Reformed, grew substantially in this era as well. Among the Dutch, a series of schisms in Holland and America led to the Christian Reformed Church (1857), a separatist and conservative body, much like the Missouri Synod Lutheran, strictly confessional and built on a substantial ethnic subculture and educational system. Many other northern European groups, such as some varieties of Mennonites, the (Methodistic) Evangelical Association and the United Brethren in Christ, the Evangelical Free church, the Swedish Evangelical Mission Covenant, and the Swedish Baptists grew in America from the immigration of this era. Most of these groups, because of their continuing doctrinal conservatism, in the later twentieth century came to be

45

classified as "evangelical." Reformed and Mennonite groups, however, because of their distinctive heritages, were often uneasy with the term.

AFRICAN AMERICAN EVANGELICALISM

Black Protestants were one of the largest American religious groups who were shaped by the evangelical heritage and preserved it the longest; but because of racial segregation that isolated them from their white counterparts, they seldom used the term "evangelical," and their experience is usually regarded as a distinct type in itself.

Christianity among Blacks

African Americans were a unique case in America, seldom paralleled in the history of any civilization. Brought to America by capitalistic Christians who treated them as though they were simply property, they were robbed of most of what gives people a sense of identity. When they were brought from Africa they had been removed from almost all ethnic and family connections, and separated from the dignity of work. They were also separated from their traditional religions so that only vestiges of those ancient practices survived. In slavery only two major factors had been available for building a positive black subculture: kinship ties and evangelical Christianity. The latter they had appropriated with appreciation, enthusiasm, and imagination, seeing in evangelicalism not just a white person's religion but a true gospel of spiritually based liberation. At the root of evangelicalism, they had found, was the Bible, and the Bible was not about white people but about all peoples for whom God had cared. To the oppressed, God had brought redemption and hope even in the times of deepest trouble.

Liberation from slavery, although truly revolutionary, did not change the social standing of black people nearly as much as might have been hoped. Even with slavery removed, the vast majority remained in the rural South. There black people had to contend with at least three other factors, any one of which was sufficient to ensure that they would remain at the lowest rung socially: lack of education, poverty, and racial prejudice. The first of these was attacked immediately after the Civil War, especially with the aid of some self-sacrificing New Englanders, and soon continued with some black leadership to provide at least modest beginnings of an educational system up to the college level. Such efforts were severely restricted by the other two factors. After the war, black people in the South were very quickly forced into economic dependence, especially in the sharecropping system. That made a rise from sheer rural poverty extremely difficult and unlikely. Absolutely sealing the social fate of the African Americans, however, was the issue of race. The central theme in the southern history of the time, as was later observed, was the absolute determination that the South remain a white person's country. For a brief time during the "Reconstruction" that followed the Civil War, blacks were guaranteed their civil rights and even participated substantially in political leadership. These roles, however, were guaranteed only by the presence of federal troops in the South. When these were finally removed in 1877 as part of a political compromise, blacks were soon put back "in their place" by a caste system that kept them apart from participation in the white-dominated society. "Jim Crow" laws demanded that they shop, eat, and travel separately from whites. Southern white church members, firmly convinced of the inferiority of the black race and reinforced in these views by growing racial prejudices in both North and South, often lent theological support to such separation and discrimination. In the southern culture at large, increasing racial hatred aggravated the plight of the black person. In the 1890s lynchings of blacks in the South took place at an average rate of three per week.

In this new, separate, and hostile setting, the black churches and Christianity played tremendously important roles. Two major contributions are distinguishable. Institutionally, the black churches were the most important agencies in providing structure and leadership to the newly separate black communities. Spiritually, the Christianity of the black people was incalculably important in their extreme circumstances in providing them with meaning, acceptance, hope, and a moral dignity that surpassed that of their evangelical white oppressors.

During slavery southern blacks had worshipped in white churches, albeit in separated areas. Freedom quickly brought accord that blacks should form their own congregations and denominations. For the whites separation was a means of institutionalizing their revulsion at dealing with Negroes on any basis that resembled equality. For the blacks, separation was essential for establishing their ecclesiastical independence from white control.

These almost universally welcomed southern black churches were virtually the only black institutions to survive Reconstruction without being seriously crippled. The growth of these churches was remarkable. They included about forty-three percent of the black population by World War I. The sphere of influence in the community was much larger than the strict membership statistics. W. E. B. DuBois in 1903 observed that "In the South, at least, practically every American Negro is a church member." DuBois added a social explanation that is generally accepted. "A proscribed people," he said, "must have a social center, and that center for this people is the Negro church." Indeed, the influence of the church in the black communities during the era seems difficult to overestimate. The ministry was virtually the only profession open to blacks, and except for the brief period of Reconstruction, was almost the only avenue there ever had been in America for black male leadership. Moreover, the churches were the only institutions that belonged fully to the black people. They were often sources of pride, as some notable edifices in southern cities testify, and in the towns and countryside they were the primary social centers for black communities. Southern black peoplehood during this era was built largely on the church. The famous remark of a rural Alabama black about his neighboring town serves as an astute, if unintended, sociological commentary. "The nationality in there," he said, "is Methodist."

The character of the Christianity in the black churches was shaped by several factors. On the surface it was much like the white Baptist and Methodist traditions out of which it had grown. But there were several differences. First of all, coming from cultures that were far closer to biblical cultures than were European-Americans, African Americans did not hear Christian teaching through the abstract categories of Greek thought and the theological controversies of the Western world. Their Christianity was more immediately biblical. "Bible-believer," rather than "evangelical," was the term used to describe their heritage. Their faith was also more spontaneous than that of their white counterparts and was marked especially by the responsive and antiphonal character of the worship services — a melodic and creative dialogue between preacher and congregation anticipating patterns later found in jazz. Moreover, although blacks and whites had in slavery listened to the same preaching, the blacks heard in the gospel different meanings than had their white oppressors. In freedom, these characteristics of their theology were articulated. Particularly, they were sensitive to the mysteries of God's providential care. In stories such as the Exodus or in the theme of the baby Jesus they saw that God cared for his people, both as a mighty warrior and as a tender friend who shared human frailties and infirmities. Hopes for heaven were prominent, as in some spirituals, yet such interests were not opposed to concern for the gospel's impact in this life. In fact, a striking factor of black Christian consciousness, contrasted with the white evangelical counterparts, is that from their vantage point of being the poor and the oppressed they heard more clearly the biblical themes of Christian responsibilities to brothers and sisters in need.

The strength of this black Christian community was tested by many of the same forces of secularization that were transforming all of America. These themes became especially prominent after the turn of the century when the great migration to the northern cities began. Francis J. Grimke, a black preacher in Washington, D.C., summarized the situation well in 1899. While demanding that the black person must be recognized as a "full-fledged citizen," and deploring the revival of "southern barbarism" manifested in recent lynch laws, Grimke maintained that the greatest dangers to his people were the social vices of materialism, drunkenness, and sexual license they faced in the cities.

Without the social supports of the close-knit rural communities, the black churches in the cities, though still predominantly traditional, were often being reshaped by the unsettled conditions and the competition of a free enterprise system. In this setting storefront churches flourished. Holiness and pentecostal groups of bewildering varieties provided channels of expression for depths of emotion among the migrants. Sects and cults flourished as well. The most famous of these was that of Father Divine (ca. 1879-1965), who claimed to be God incarnate and who rose to fame in Brooklyn and Harlem during the 1920s and 1930s. Such extravagances, though widely publicized, should not be exaggerated. Nearly two-thirds of black church membership was Baptist, and most of the other third was from the Methodist tradition. The center of black life was still the church, not only in the rural South, but even in the cities of the North to which the balance of the population was shifting. The churches, though battered during the jazz age, were still forces to be contended with.

THE EMERGENCE OF FUNDAMENTALISM

Wars are the catalysts of history. They precipitate and accelerate trends already present in a culture. World War I had an especially momentous impact on American life. Until this time the United States had stayed off the center stage of world affairs. Prewar America, despite its problems of assimilating so many diverse peoples, had been remarkably optimistic. No challenge was too great to be mastered by American idealism and know-how. Americans threw all their confidence and moral fervor into the war effort, and they succeeded. Yet the success was confined very largely to the battlefield. Despite some expectations to the contrary, war was not a sanctifying experience. Abroad, the crusade to "make America safe for democracy" was soon left in a shambles. At home the war unleashed the forces of secularization that brought the jazz age. It also sparked an era of bitterness and reaction. American idealism was overwhelmed by dissension. Although rearguard actions were fought to keep America Protestant, the fact of the matter was that the age was over when the United States was in any significant sense a bastion of "Christendom."

While every major Christian group in American was significantly changed by the war, the impact on the culturally dominant white Protestant community probably was the most intense. The cultural changes associated with the war and its aftermath sent this community reeling for two decades, and, when it recovered to some extent after World War II, it was not the same.

Once America entered the European war in the spring of 1917, few clergy could resist the overwhelming patriotic impulse that swept the country. Some identified Christianity and Americanism completely. "Christianity and Patriotism are synonymous terms, " said evangelist Billy Sunday directly, "and hell and traitors are synonymous." Sunday (1862-1935) was just at the height of his fame when the war broke out, and he incorporated the war in his message with extravagant enthusiasm. Of all the major American evangelists such as Finney, Moody, Sunday, and Graham, Billy Sunday was the greatest showman. An ex-baseball player, his sermons were filled with acrobatics, jumping, falling, whirling, and sliding. When flushed with patriotism, he would end his sermon by jumping on top of the pulpit and waving the American flag.

Except for style, most theological liberals had nothing to concede to conservatives on the patriotic front. Whereas evangelists such as Sunday mixed a patriotic folk religion with their Christianity, liberals had a deeper theological stake in the war to "make the world safe for democracy." The most modernistic versions of their gospel saw God as working through the progress of civilization, especially democratic civilization as found in America. The war was then for them quite explicitly a sacred cause. So said Shailer Mathews, dean of the University of Chicago Divinity School, in a characteristic statement: "For an American to refuse to share in the present war . . . is not Christian."

Among both conservative and liberal Christians, moderates on the war issue wrestled with the moral dilemmas involved. The pressures of public opinion, however, forced most nonenthusiasts into a discreet silence. Many, including preachers and theologians, were ready to cast the first stone at a suspected slacker. At the University of Chicago Divinity School, for instance, dispensational premillennialism (which rejected the equation of the progress of the kingdom and the progress of democratic society) was considered subversive to the war effort and subjected to scathing attacks.

Such pressures soon brought almost everyone into line with extravagant avowals of their patriotism. By 1918 such sentiments were aided by widely circulated and accepted atrocity stories about Germany, convincing many that the war was a matter of Christian civilization versus bloodthirsty and barbaric huns. A leader in creating this belief was the Rev. Newell Dwight Hillis, pastor of Henry Ward Beecher's old church, Plymouth Congregational in Brooklyn. During 1917 Hillis lectured some four hundred times on German atrocities, inflaming his audiences with stories of how German soldiers typically raped and then mutilated innocent women. He claimed that the Kaiser had given every soldier explicit license to "commit any crime he may desire." (One of the worst consequences of this hysteria only became apparent much later, when journalists who reported Hitler's atrocities were ignored and their accounts discredited as nothing more than wartime propaganda.)

The main effect at the time, however, was to create American hatred of anything German. The teaching of the German language was forbidden in some public schools, and in many places church services in any language other than English were regarded as evidence of insufficient patriotism. Public opinion against the use of foreign languages in religious services during the war together with pressure to demonstrate total American-ism were important factors in hastening the Americanization of many Catholics, Protestants, and Orthodox who had re-cently immigrated.

The Aftermath

When the war ended in November 1918 the crusading zeal of the nation had not yet reached its crest. The extreme patri-otism built up by the wartime propaganda was reinforced by the decisive successes of the American armies. But then as enthusiasm was still building, the sudden peace left the nation at an extreme psychological pitch but no longer with a clearly defined enemy. During the next years, the high-pitched en-thusiasm was mixed with the dregs of bitterness, suspicion, and hatred. As usual, the churches played a central role.

At first the overwhelming mood in most of the churches was a sense of unity and idealism. The most dramatic mani-festation of this mood was the final victory of Prohibition. During 1917 this movement, which had been steadily growing for decades, suddenly emerged victorious in the midst of the wartime enthusiasm. Many Protestants, Catholics, and pro-gressives united in this remarkable effort to clean up the home front. Several laws banning the manufacture or sale of alcoholic beverages were quickly passed, soon followed by the Eigh-teenth Amendment, which only reaffirmed the accomplished fact when it finally went into effect in 1919. The apparent triumph of this social experiment was largely a tribute to the Christian idealism of the age.

The war at first had a unifying effect. Among Protestants zeal for Christian unity and worldwide reform ran especially high. The most important effort to organize this zeal was the massive interdenominational Interchurch World Movement, launched immediately after the war. This movement, reflecting the same enthusiasm that earlier had inspired the Men and Religion Forward Movement, was designed to unite Christian benevolent, missionary, and spiritual efforts throughout the world. Amid talk of actual church union, the leaders of the movement shared a "vision of a united church uniting a divided world."

By the summer of 1920 the Interchurch World Movement was in a shambles. Conservative opposition brought about a fate much like that of the League of Nations, which President Woodrow Wilson had proposed with such high hopes, only to have the United States itself in 1920 refuse to join.

In the churches, as in the nation generally, the idealism of World War I was very quickly overshadowed by a growing mood of bitter reaction. When the war ended abruptly it seemed as though a considerable element of the American people needed to find new enemies on whom to vent their superheated emotions. The Marxist revolution in Russia in 1917 together with labor unrest and a series of frightening terrorist bombings fueled the "Red Scare" during 1919 in which much of the nation was gripped with fears of communist infiltration and uprising. More directly involved with the churches was the revival of the Ku Klux Klan. Reorganized in 1915, this antiblack organization extended its range of hatreds to include Catholics, Jews, and non-Nordic people generally. If the war had accelerated the assimilation of these non-Nordic groups into the mainstream of American life, its aftermath accelerated the reactions and prejudices against them among many northern European Americans. By 1923 the Klan had reached a peak membership of nearly three million. While not identified directly with any one denomination or Protestant movement, and disclaimed by liberals and conservatives alike, the Klan claimed explicitly to be Protestant. It appropriated Christian teaching, hymns, and symbols, and represented a notable segment of the professing Protestant community. The symbol of the flaming cross perhaps best captures the way in which this movement, like the Nazi movement in Germany

54

between the wars, represented an amalgamation of Christian tradition with nationalistic folk religion, self-interest, and hatred.

The Klan, of course, did not represent the vast majority of American Protestants either in the South or the North. It was, however, an extreme manifestation of tendencies that in milder forms were more pervasive within the dominant American community. Specifically, sentiments were strong against "foreigners." Economically they seemed to be a threat, and socially they were at the center of urban problems. Moreover, religiously and culturally their continued influx would spell the end of Protestant Anglo-Saxon dominance. Together, such sentiments led to immigration restrictions after the war, culminating in the Johnson-Reed Act of 1924, which placed severe quotas on the proportions of the U.S. population as it had been in 1890. Such efforts struck directly at the growth of the Jewish, southern and eastern European Catholic, and Orthodox communities.

All American religious communities faced serious and disconcerting challenges on another front during the 1920s. The war had accelerated and brought out into the open the secularization that had been growing in American life. Whereas in 1900 one might have talked about religion in polite company but never would have dared mention sex, by the 1920s the opposite was often the case. This "revolution in morals" was especially apparent in the cities and in the eastern and educated culture that dominated the American media. The modern tabloid newspaper, headlined with sensational and suggestive stories, began in 1919. The movies made the most of sex stars. Semiserious popular literature was filled with discussions of Freud, Freudianism, and the importance of freedom of expression. Modern advertising exploited the new freedom, selling soap, as it was remarked, as though it were an aphrodisiac. Along with this change in the popular culture came the virtual collapse of communal enforcement of standards of personal behavior that had been among the mainstays of the churches. Women smoked in public, did not always cover their knees (even in church), and refused to follow the domestic examples of their mothers. Dancing, which had long been a taboo for many Protestants, now was an integral part of social acceptability in the age of the flapper. While some church leaders simply conceded the issue and even brought dancing into church youth group meetings, others were horrified. The new dances, one conservative Southern Methodist bishop complained, brought "the bodies of men and women in unusual relations to each other." The rumble seats of the new automobiles did the same. Despite the passage of Prohibition, then, the battle to enforce traditional Victorian and Methodistic mores was a losing one.

Such a climate of crisis brought extreme conflict of opinion in many Protestant churches. Many liberals remained optimistic and saw the breakdown of traditions as opportunity for building a new liberal Christian consensus. Conservatives, on the other hand, reacted strongly. So the same diverse postwar forces that produced both the Interchurch World Movement and the revival of the Klan, the legal triumph of Prohibition and the actual triumph of a general revolution against traditional Protestant mores, brought deep division over serious theological and ecclesiastical issues. These differences had long been developing. Both liberalism and sizable conservative countermovements had been building for a generation; but before the war the activism of the era had overshadowed theological debates and relative peace had been preserved. The war and postwar crisis, however, forced each party to confront the others and to see how widely they actually differed in their visions for the churches and for American culture.

Fundamentalists Versus Modernists

The outstanding manifestation of this mutual discovery was the fundamentalist-modernist controversy that dominated much of the religious news of the 1920s. It would be difficult to say who fired the first shot in this conflict since by the end of World War I major salvos were being issued from both sides.

Liberals were more aggressive than previously in organizing for unity and action and in specifically attacking their conservative opponents. Conservatives, likewise, were organizing, most notably in the founding in 1919 of the World's Christian Fundamentals Association, a dispensationalist-premillennialist group organized to combat modernism. The next year conservatives in the Northern Baptist Convention instituted a "Fundamentals" conference to muster opposition to liberalism in that denomination. The term "fundamentalist," originated on this occasion, when Curtis Lee Laws, conservative editor of the Baptist paper *The Watchman-Examiner,* coined it to describe those ready "to do battle royal for the Fundamentals." Soon the term caught on to describe all sorts of American Protestants who were willing to wage ecclesiastical and theological war against modernism in theology and the cultural changes that modernists celebrated.

The fundamentalist forces of the 1920s were formidable because they represented a coalition of conservative Protestants that had been growing for some time. At the center of this coalition were dispensationalist premillennialists who had been promoting dispensationalist teachings for nearly half a century through prophecy conferences, Bible institutes, evangelistic campaigns, and the *Scofield Reference Bible* (1909). These same leaders had promoted a wider coalition with the publication and wide, free distribution of *The Fundamentals,* twelve paperback volumes containing defenses of fundamental doctrines by a variety of American and British conservative writers.

In the early 1920s the conflict mushroomed in Protestant churches as well as in the culture generally. In major denominations and their mission fields conservatives attempted to forestall the advances of modernism by various types of legislation designed to require adherence to fundamental doctrines of traditional supernaturalistic Christianity. On foreign mission fields, where evangelicals considered the very salvation of souls to be at stake, conservative versus liberal rivalries were especially intense, and these conflicts were reflected in the crisis at home. Such conflicts were especially severe in denominations where fundamentalism and liberalism were represented by parties of almost equal strength. The Northern Baptist Convention and the (northern) Presbyterian Church in the U.S.A. were the centers of denominational controversy. Among the Disciples of Christ a parallel conflict was waged between liberals and Disciples traditionalists, leading to a virtual separation of the two parties by the mid-1920s. The Protestant Episcopal church and the Northern Methodists experienced minor fundamentalist furors during this same era, but in these denominations liberalism and moderation were so far advanced that fundamentalists had little chance of success. The same was true of Congregationalists, among whom there was no real controversy. In the South, by contrast, conservatives were so dominant that little controversy was necessary to bring endorsements from such denominations as the Southern Baptist Convention and the (southern) Presbyterian Church in the U.S. of their northern "fundamentalist" counterparts. Ever since the Civil War most southerners had been against liberalism and modernism, which they associated with Yankee culture.

In the battle for the denominations the leading spokesperson for the fundamentalist-conservative coalition was Presbyterian J. Gresham Machen, Professor of New Testament at Princeton Theological Seminary. In *Christianity and Liberalism* (1923), Machen argued that since the new liberalism denied that human salvation was dependent on the historical fact that Christ had died to atone for human sins, such liberalism was not Christianity at all, but a new religion. It was essentially a faith in humanity even though it used Christian language and symbolism. In honesty, he said, liberals should withdraw from churches that had been founded on a very different basis of biblical Christianity. Liberals responded in kind, arguing that they were preserving the essence of Christianity and that conservatives were endorsing only "theories" about what the Bible taught. Most importantly, liberals took their stand on the question of tolerance. Since even within the denominations such as the Northern Baptist and northern Presbyterian, where the

58

contests were most heated, most American Protestants were neither modernists nor militant fundamentalists, overtures for peace and tolerance often could command substantial support. So while in these denominations fundamentalists won some token victories, by 1926 it became clear that policies of inclusiveness and tolerance would prevail.

In the meantime, the fundamentalist controversy had gained additional attention on the cultural front as fundamentalists organized to save the whole of American society from "infidelity." World War I had produced among many conservative evangelicals both a sense of crisis over the revolution in morals and a renewed concern for the welfare of civilization. For one thing, the war had coincided with the Marxist revolution of 1917 that brought widespread fear of the spread of a frankly atheistic political system. Even more to the point, so far as American culture was concerned, was the model of Germany. German civilization during the war was portrayed as the essence of barbarism, despite its strongly Christian heritage. Could the same thing happen here? The strong winds of change suggested that it could.

The central symbol organizing fears over the demise of American culture became biological evolution. German culture, antievolutionists loudly proclaimed, had been ruined by the evolutionary "might-makes-right" philosophy of Friedrich Nietzsche. Darwinism, moreover, was essentially atheistic, and hence its spread would contribute to the erosion of American morality. Accordingly, soon after the war fundamentalists began organizing vigorous campaigns against the teaching of biological evolution in America's public schools. This effort was greatly aided when in 1920 William Jennings Bryan, three times Democratic candidate for president and one of the nation's greatest orators, entered the fray against Darwinism. Fundamentalist antievolution efforts were essentially political and so attracted a constituency wider than the nucleus of theologically conservative evangelical Protestants. By the middle of the decade laws banning the teaching of evolution in public schools had been passed in a number of southern states, and legislation was pending in numbers of others. These efforts led to the famous Scopes Trial testing the Tennessee antievolution law in 1925, an event that both thrust fundamentalism into worldwide attention and brought about its decline as an effective national force. John T. Scopes, a young high-school teacher who admitted to teaching biological evolution, was brought to trial and defended by famed criminal lawyer Clarence Darrow. William Jennings Bryan volunteered to aid the prosecution, thus bringing a dramatic showdown between fundamentalism and modern scepticism. The event was comparable to Lindbergh's transatlantic flight in the amount of press coverage and ballyhoo.

Although the outcome of the trial was indecisive and the law stood, the rural setting and the press's caricatures of fundamentalists as rubes and hicks discredited fundamentalism and made it difficult to pursue further the serious aspects of the movement. After 1925 fundamentalists had difficulty gaining national attention except when some of their movement were involved in extreme or bizarre efforts. For instance, one of the most highly publicized religious figures of the era was evangelist Aimee Semple McPherson. She was not strictly a fundamentalist in the sense of being involved in the antimodernist campaigns, but was a pentecostal emphasizing healing and the gift of tongues. In 1926, in a widely publicized and sensational event, she disappeared for a month, claiming to have been kidnapped. Others accused her of scandal, but she survived the episode more popular than ever, founding in Los Angeles in 1927 her own denomination, the International Church of the Foursquare Gospel.

Although such sensations clouded the image of revivalist Protestantism, the movement continued to grow in many varieties outside the mainstream of Protestant church life. In the meantime, the mainstream denominations themselves had been hurt by the lengthy fundamentalist controversies and by their own lack of clear direction.

While the fundamentalist-modernist controversy dominated Protestantism and most of the religious news of the decade, various non-Protestant groups were establishing stronger footholds as permanent parts of American culture and religion.

The most dramatic manifestation of these gains was the nomination of Al Smith, a Catholic, as Democratic candidate for president in 1928. Smith's campaign, however, elicited from conservative Protestants a barrage of polemics against Catholicism. "Tomorrow we might have Smith," they reasoned, "the next day the Pope." Such accusations turned votes, but not the election, which almost certainly would have gone to Herbert Hoover in any case. This episode, however, as was also true of the support of immigration restriction earlier in the decade, indicated that many Protestants were not yet willing to give up the idea that America was a Protestant land.

Conservative Protestant opposition to the Smith campaign was the last major appearance of fundamentalism in American public life during the 1920s. Soon it looked to be the last hurrah for fundamentalism altogether. Fundamentalism seemed to be in disarray, and most observers assumed that it had burned itself out and would soon disappear forever. Critics typically assumed that fundamentalism was largely the product of rural culture and that once modern education spread it would lose its social base.

In fact, however, fundamentalism was not disappearing but realigning. Not being able to control either the major northern denominations nor the political culture, fundamentalists continued to do what they did best, evangelize and build up local churches. For evangelization, they long had been masters of the mass media and so adapted quickly to radio. Locally their individual churches and agencies grew, even if slowed by the financial pressures of the depression of the early 1930s. Some fundamentalists separated into their own churches, while other conservatives quietly remained in major denominations. Their national organizations, either within denominations or in politics, declined; but vigor at the local level ensured that this segment of American Protestantism was one of the few that was growing during the 1930s. It was not until decades later, when fundamentalists and their evangelical heirs reemerged in American life, that many observers noticed this growth or took it seriously.

61

2. Evangelicalism since 1930: Unity and Diversity

I F THE NEW EVANGELICALISM that eventually emerged as heir to the original fundamentalist coalition of the 1920s ever had a chance of achieving some real working unity it would have centered around Billy Graham in his prime. Carl F. H. Henry, once one of Graham's lieutenants, looking back in 1980 observed, "During the 1960s I somewhat romanced the possibility that a vast evangelical alliance might arise in the United States to coordinate effectively a national impact in evangelism, education, publication and sociopolitical action." Billy Graham had decisively broken with the separatist fundamentalists, had made inroads into the major denominations, was immensely popular, and stood almost alone as a recognized evangelical leader. Henry and some of his intellectual cohorts, often known at the time as "new evangelicals" or "neo-evangelicals," had provided the movement with some ideological leadership. *Christianity Today,* under Henry's editorship, modeled itself after *The Christian Century* but had a larger circulation. The neo-evangelicals and Graham even talked seriously about founding an evangelical university in the New York City area. The movement was advancing on a number of fronts and Henry could plausibly imagine that the core group of new evangelical reformers of fundamentalism could successfully mobilize a cohesive united evangelical front, reminiscent of the heyday of American evangelicalism in the nineteenth century.

"By the early 1970s," Henry recollected, "the prospect of a massive evangelical alliance seemed annually more remote, and by mid-decade it was gone."[1] Evangelicalism was thriving more than ever and awareness of it was reentering the national consciousness. Yet by 1976, when *Newsweek* proclaimed "The Year of the Evangelical," the hopes of the neo-evangelicals for unity under their leadership had dissipated. Having a Southern Baptist and a Democrat elected to the White House did not advance their party's cause. In addition, for them 1976 brought increasingly open internal strife, centered on "the battle for the Bible." As evangelicals gained some of the national prestige they had once only dreamed of, the neo-evangelical leaders could no longer agree among themselves as to what an evangelical was.

Certainly one of the most remarkable developments in American religion since 1930 has been the reemergence of evangelicalism as a force in American culture. Probably it is the one least likely to have been predicted in 1930. Fundamentalism appeared to have been defeated in those major northern denominations in which it had raised serious challenges during the 1920s, and progressives were in control. All that remained to be carried out, according to prevailing sociological theories, were mopping-up operations. Conservative religion would die out as modernity advanced. The backward South would become more like the industrialized North. Fundamentalists had their own version of this theory, expecting secularization to advance steadily in churches and culture until Christ returned. Few thought the South would rise again to set the religious-cultural tone for much of the nation.[2] Few would have thought

1. Carl F. H. Henry, "American Evangelicals in a Turning Time," *The Christian Century* ("How My Mind Has Changed" series), November 5, 1980, p. 1060.
2. This important feature of recent evangelical developments is discussed by Grant Wacker, "Uneasy in Zion: Evangelicals in Postmodern

that fifty years later the progressive denominations would be in a state of steady decline, while evangelical and conservative groups would be flourishing.

The "neo-evangelical" reformers of fundamentalism were among the first to anticipate the possibility of an evangelical resurgence. Already in the 1940s they were talking gradiloquently not only about such a comeback, but even about "the restating of the fundamental thesis and principles of a Western culture"[3] and, as Carl Henry put it, "remaking the modern mind."[4] They were convinced that if the voice of fundamentalism could be tempered slightly, evangelical Christianity could "win America."[5] They saw themselves as standing in the tradition of Dwight L. Moody, Charles Finney, Jonathan Edwards, and George Whitefield, representing the long-standing transdenominational center of the American evangelical tradition. An American evangelicalism once again more or less organized, they thought, could still be a formidable force in American culture and a challenge to the dominant trends toward secularism in the West.

The success that the movement had attained by the 1970s was only partly what its leaders had envisioned. The movement got far beyond their control and grew as the result of forces never anticipated in their plans. The extent to which their plans actually shaped the movement is difficult to estimate. It is important not to mistake a few prominent spokespersons for a movement. Nonetheless, by focusing first on these visionaries and organizers, we can find a window through which to see the larger movement, both as it fit their vision and as it did not.

Given the bewildering diversity of American evangel-

Society," in George Marsden, ed., *Evangelicalism and Modern America* (Grand Rapids: Eerdmans, 1984), pp. 17-28.

3. Harold J. Ockenga, "The Challenge to the Christian Culture of the West," First Opening Convocation address, Fuller Theological Seminary, Pasadena, California, October 1, 1947, pamphlet.

4. Carl F. H. Henry, *Remaking the Modern Mind* (Grand Rapids: Eerdmans, 1946).

5. Harold J. Ockenga, "Can Christians Win America?," *Christian Life and Times*, June 1947, pp. 13-15.

icalism, it might seem remarkable that any one party would have supposed it could provide unifying leadership. Timothy L. Smith has argued, with some persuasiveness, that evangelicalism is like a kaleidoscope. It is made up of fragments as diverse as black pentecostals, Mennonite peace churches, Episcopal charismatics, Nazarenes, and Southern Baptists. It is a grouping for which no one party could presume to speak.[6] From this perspective, one could regard evangelicalism as a unity only in a very broad sense. Evangelicals might agree in a general way on the essentials of evangelicalism: "that the sole authority in religion is the Bible and the sole means of salvation is a life-transforming experience wrought by the Holy Spirit through Faith in Jesus Christ."[7] Other than that, they represent largely independent, even if related, traditions.[8]

Despite the general validity of these observations, which must qualify any talk about a single "evangelicalism," twentieth-century American evangelicalism has had more unity than its denominational diversity might suggest. This degree of unity grows not only out of a common basic profession but also out of a considerable common heritage and experience. Even most black Protestants, who have been almost entirely separated from whites since the Civil War, have enough common heritage to be readily identifiable as "evangelical," though they seldom use the word. As for white evangelicals, with whom this essay is primarily concerned, the bondings of their common heritage were reinforced during the first half of the twentieth century by the shared experiences of most of them in fundamentalist reactions against "modernist" theological innovations and certain cultural changes.

6. Timothy L. Smith, "The Evangelical Kaleidoscope and the Call to Christian Unity," *Christian Scholar's Review* 15/2 (1986), 125-40.
7. Grant Wacker, *Augustus H. Strong and the Dilemma of Historical Consciousness* (Macon, GA: Mercer University Press, 1985), p. 17. This is not an exhaustive definition, but it is economical and carefully framed.
8. The conceptual questions involved in relating the whole to the parts of evangelicalism are discussed by George Marsden, "The Evangelical Denomination," in Marsden, ed., *Evangelicalism and Modern America*, pp. vii-xix.

In the 1930s "evangelicalism" was not a term much used in American religious life. The white Protestant world was still dominated by the mainline denominations, and these were divided by wars between "fundamentalists" and their sympathizers and "modernists" and their sympathizers. Both sides had earlier claimed the appellation "evangelical," so that it was no longer of much use to either. Strictly speaking, most American Protestants, clergy as well as laypeople, were neither fundamentalists nor modernists, but were located somewhere in between. The fundamentalist/modernist wars, however, had forced many such moderates to choose sides. In the North, most clerics favored tolerance of modernism and most laypeople did not want a fight. In the South, most of both groups were willing to hold the line with the fundamentalists.

By the 1930s the northern white churches were undergoing realignment,[9] as fundamentalists relocated and built their own networks of separate institutions. Uncounted numbers of fundamentalists left the major denominations to join or to found independent local Bible churches, or they forsook a more liberal denomination for a smaller, more conservative one. Most fundamentalists, nonetheless, remained quietly within the major denominations, hoping to work within existing structures, especially through conservative local churches. At the same time they increasingly gave their support to a growing network of trans-denominational fundamentalist evangelistic agencies.[10]

Fundamentalism embodied two paradoxical impulses that its advocates always had difficulty reconciling. What chiefly distinguished fundamentalism from earlier evangelicalism was its militancy toward modernist theology and cultural change. Metaphors of warfare dominated its thinking, and the rhetoric of "no compromise" often precipitated denominational show-

9. The classic exposition of the condition of the mainline churches during this era is Robert T. Handy, "The American Religious Depression, 1925-1935," *Church History* 29 (1960), 2-16.

10. Joel A. Carpenter, "Fundamentalist Institutions and the Rise of Evangelical Protestantism, 1929-1942," *Church History* 49/1 (March 1980), 62-75.

downs. Once it became apparent after 1925, however, that fundamentalists could not control the major northern denominations,[11] the logic of their no-compromise position pointed toward separatism. Dispensational premillennial interpretations of history, which had spread widely among fundamentalists, supported this separatist tendency. Dispensationalism taught the apostasy of the major churches of "Christendom" as part of a steady cultural degeneration during the present "church age." By the 1930s the strictest fundamentalists increasingly were proclaiming the duty of ecclesiastical separatism.

Fundamentalism, however, also incorporated a positive impulse that often worked at cross-purposes with this negativism. Antedating fundamentalist antimodernism was the evangelical revivalist tradition out of which fundamentalism had grown. The overriding preoccupation of this tradition was the saving of souls. Any responsible means to promote this end was approved. As American revivalism developed, it did so with basically sympathetic ambivalence toward the major denominations. To be sure, part of the appeal of the revival impulse was based on dissatisfaction with what the denominations were doing. A few revivalists, such as Alexander Campbell, founded their own denominations, but the most successful, such as Charles Finney and Dwight Moody, worked alongside the respected denominations, often building their own evangelistic organizations to supplement denominational efforts. The evangelical denominations, for their part, encouraged revivalism and promoted it through both denominational and extradenominational agencies.

The negative fundamentalist impulse in the 1930s to abandon the major denominations was countered by its prior, ongoing agenda to win America and the world for Christ. This agenda seemed to require believers in "the fundamentals" to hold on to

11. The fundamentalist developments during the earlier era are discussed in Chapter 1 and in more detail in George Marsden, *Fundamentalism and American Culture: The Shaping of Twentieth-Century Evangelicalism, 1870-1925* (New York: Oxford University Press, 1980).

their entrenched positions in the respected denominations. If they gave up all connections with these denominations, how could they get a hearing to win the nation? Though most fundamentalists by the 1930s had put aside the discouraging business of political programs in favor of emphasizing soul winning, they still (contrary to the cultural pessimism of dispensational teaching) entertained at least lingering aspirations to a wider social, spiritual, and moral influence such as evangelicals had enjoyed only a generation earlier. Retaining some connections with the major denominations suited this positive strategy.

This positive strategy involved only a halfway separation of most fundamentalists from the denominational mainstream. While some fundamentalists built new institutions that were strictly separatist, more were building institutions that were in practice separate, but had not in theory repudiated the mainstream. During the 1930s the lines between these two kinds of separatism were not always clear. Some leading fundamentalists insisted on repudiating old-line denominations. Others, equally prominent, stayed in. The situation was fluid, so that for most groups in the transdenominational coalition separatism was not yet a test of faith.

In this ecclesiastically unsettled atmosphere, fundamentalists moved ahead by building their network of largely evangelistic agencies. The radio offered a particularly effective way to build up ministries that, consistent with long-standing revivalist practice, ignored denominational considerations.

By the early 1940s, Charles E. Fuller of "The Old-Fashioned Revival Hour" had gained the largest radio audience in the country. In the 1920s Fuller had been a typical fundamentalist militant and had split a local Presbyterian congregation to form his own group; but by the time he became a national figure, he had adopted the positive fundamentalist stance of refusing to engage in controversy or to make separatism a test of orthodoxy.[12]

---

12. Daniel P. Fuller, *Give the Winds a Mighty Voice: The Story of Charles E. Fuller* (Waco, TX: Word Books, 1972).

By the early 1940s fundamentalists, typically working through recently formed organizations, were seeing signs of revival on a number of fronts. Most notably successful of the new organizations was Youth for Christ. During World War II youth evangelists such as Jack Wyrtzen and Percy Crawford had sponsored remarkably successful mass rallies in American cities, notably New York and Chicago. In 1945 Youth for Christ International was organized to consolidate a considerable revival. During its first year, Youth for Christ sponsored nearly 900 rallies nationwide, with about one million constituents.[13] The new organization chose a young graduate of Wheaton College, Billy Graham, as its first full-time evangelist. By the end of the decade, Graham carried the revival movement to massive national success.

Graham's base was a network of positive fundamentalists who had been organizing for such a revival throughout the 1940s. The most visible institutional manifestation of this network was the National Association of Evangelicals, founded in 1942 as a loose affiliation of diverse evangelical denominations and individuals, primarily to promote evangelism. The NAE was the national outgrowth of the earlier New England Fellowship, headed by J. Elwin Wright. Harold John Ockenga, a former student of the scholarly J. Gresham Machen and pastor of the Park Street Congregational Church in Boston, became the chief organizer of the NAE and also headed a number of other important agencies founded during the next two decades. At the center of these organizations was a group of people, predominantly Baptist and Presbyterian, most of whom had connections with institutions such as Wheaton College, Moody Bible Institute, Dallas Theological Seminary, Gordon College and Seminary in Boston, and those followers of Machen who were not strict separatists.

This group built up a broad constituency, as is evident

13. Joel A. Carpenter, "From Fundamentalism to the New Evangelical Coalition," in Marsden, ed., *Evangelicalism and Modern America*, p. 15.

from the NAE, which by 1947 included thirty small denominations, representing 1,300,000 members. The NAE leadership reflected the more or less mainstream heritage of fundamentalism. Many of its leaders still belonged to major denominations. Working from this broad fundamentalist base, they also brought in some evangelical groups that had been on the periphery of the earlier fundamentalist movement. Groups with ethnic origins, such as the Swedish Baptists and the Evangelical Free Church, found the national movement a congenial form of Americanization. Holiness groups, such as the Nazarenes and the Wesleyan Methodists, found their distinctive emphases being reshaped by the fundamentalist-led movement. And even some pentecostal denominations, which had been pariahs among the earlier negative fundamentalists, were invited into the fellowship of the positive movement. The Southern Baptist Convention, which would have swelled the numbers of the NAE immensely, had representatives at some early meetings but had too distinct an identity to join the movement. The smaller Christian Reformed Church joined and then left the NAE, but some of its leaders were always important contributors to the movement. William B. Eerdmans, for instance, became its most respected publisher. Missouri Synod Lutherans, by contrast, usually remained more aloof from such versions of Americanization.[14]

The constituency of this emerging movement was, however, considerably larger than the numbers of people who could be counted in its organizations. The vast audiences who listened to Charles E. Fuller, or later to Billy Graham, were at least part-time supporters of the network and were being shaped by its message. Local radio stations, such as WMBI at the Moody Bible Institute in Chicago, similarly kept people

14. Ibid., pp. 13-14. Also see Joe Carpenter, "The Fundamentalist Leaven and the Rise of an Evangelical United Front," in Leonard Sweet, ed., *The Evangelical Tradition in America* (Macon, GA: Mercer University Press, 1984), pp. 257-88, for an important discussion of these interrelationships.

from many denominations in the positive fundamentalist orbit. Most of these people, no doubt, belonged to the major denominations. On the West Coast, for instance, the movement long had substantial support from the large and pivotal conservative Presbyterian congregations.

Although all fundamentalists had sought national revival, the stricter militants were becoming increasingly uneasy about the alliances being forged during the positive fundamentalist resurgence of the 1940s. The most vocal spokesman for this more separatist view was Carl McIntire, another former Machen student and an indefatigable organizer of opposition movements. In 1941, apparently anticipating the formation of the NAE, McIntire founded the American Council of Christian Churches on a strict fundamentalist basis—no Pentecostals and, especially, no denominations (or their members) affiliated with the Federal Council of Churches. McIntire's strictness kept his organizations small, but his vigorous promotions through publications and radio and his sensational attacks on liberals and their agencies, often emphasizing communist connections, gave him disproportional influence. During the 1940s, however, it was not clear to the heirs of fundamentalism that a split was shaping up over the relative importance of the negative and the positive components of their heritage. Both sides had some of each. Efforts were made, for instance, to merge the American Council and the NAE, and a few people belonged to both.[15]

The issues that were emerging, however, were not just negative versus positive or separatist versus inclusivist. Some ideological questions were important as well, above all the role of dispensational premillennialism in the movement. During the 1930s this doctrine was taught in the overwhelming majority of fundamentalist (and pentecostal) churches. Dispensationalism's pessimistic view of the prevailing culture en-

15. For further discussion of these developments see George Marsden, *Reforming Fundamentalism: Fuller Seminary and the New Evangelicalism* (Grand Rapids: Eerdmans, 1987).

couraged a deemphasis on social causes in the movement. Dispensationalism's negative estimate of major churches encouraged separatism.[16]

As part of the effort for an American and world revival after World War II, a group of positive fundamentalist intellectuals began organizing a move away from dispensationalist emphases. With America's emergence into world leadership after the war, they saw a unique opportunity for reconstituting Christian civilization, if America's evangelical tradition could be revived. To attain this ambitious goal, they recognized that it would be necessary to build on fundamentalism's claim to stand in the broad tradition of Augustinian orthodoxy, rather than to promote the more narrow dispensationalist teachings of recent invention. They also deplored fundamentalism's emphasis on personal ethical prohibitions at the expense of a positive social program, a theme enunciated in Carl Henry's *Uneasy Conscience of Modern Fundamentalism* in 1947. They were embarrassed, furthermore, by the anti-intellectualism that had come to be associated with dispensational fundamentalism, which had been promoted primarily through Bible institutes and pragmatic popularizers.

Their most notable effort to counter such trends was the founding of Fuller Theological Seminary in Pasadena, California, in 1947. Charles E. Fuller provided the early funding but left most of the management of the institution to the intellectuals, headed by Harold Ockenga as president and including among its early faculty an impressive lineup: Carl Henry, Edward J. Carnell, Wilbur M. Smith, Everett Harrison, Gleason Archer, Harold Lindsell, George E. Ladd, Daniel Fuller, and Paul K. Jewett. Though the Fuller faculty deemphasized dispensationalism, they did not immediately repudiate their fundamentalist heritage. They were sincerely dedicated to Charles Fuller's ideal of positive evangelism and were close associates of Billy Graham (who eventually became a trustee). The school paid its sincere respects to fundamentalist doctrinal

16. The cultural implications of dispensational teaching are discussed in Marsden, *Fundamentalism and American Culture.*

militancy, as well, by requiring creedal assent to the inerrancy of Scripture.[17]

During the 1950s, Billy Graham's success was rapidly changing the status of this predominantly positive evangelicalism that had been growing out of fundamentalism. Graham's vast popular appeal gave him virtual independence. The election of Eisenhower and Nixon in 1952 gave him entry to the White House. Support from politically conservative business leaders, most notably J. Howard Pew of Sun Oil, added to his resources, though Graham played down the political implications of his connections.[18]

Most importantly, Graham's move toward the respectable centers of American life precipitated a definitive split with the hardline fundamentalists in 1957. For his New York City crusade, Graham accepted the sponsorship of the local Protestant Council of Churches. Strict fundamentalists were deeply offended by this cooperation with liberals and they anathematized Graham.[19] In the aftermath of the resulting schism within the coalition, "fundamentalism" came to be a term used almost solely by those who demanded ecclesiastical separatism. They called their former allies "neo-evangelicals," picking up on the term "new evangelicalism" coined earlier by Ockenga. Others in the reforming group called themselves simply "evangelical," the term that eventually became common usage both for them and for the wider movement.

Recognizing that the emerging movement needed some intellectual guidance, Graham sponsored the establishment of *Christianity Today* under the editorship of Carl Henry. Ockenga was the chairman of the board and Pew the chief financial supporter. Most of the pieces were now in place for promoting their vision of a movement that would not only evangelize the

17. See note 15.
18. Richard V. Pierard, "Billy Graham and the U. S. Presidency," *Journal of Church and State* 22 (Winter 1980), 107-27.
19. This split is ably discussed by Butler Farley Porter, Jr., "Billy Graham and the End of Evangelical Unity" (Ph.D. dissertation, University of Florida, 1976).

nation but would also lay the foundations for a unified evangelical social and intellectual program. Perhaps the high-water mark in their efforts to organize a culturally significant and coherent evangelistic coalition came in 1967 with their sponsorship of the World Congress on Evangelism, a notable display of unity among most of the main evangelical leaders from America and around the world. The congress witnessed a feature of the American evangelical coalition that had been important since the nineteenth century: it was part of a wider transatlantic movement with major missionary ties.

By 1967, however, it was becoming impossible to regard American evangelicalism as a single coalition with a more or less unified and recognized leadership. In part the reason for this was negative, the result of an internal crisis. The core ex-fundamentalist movement that the neo-evangelicals hoped to speak for was splitting apart. The political issues of the 1960s were becoming sources of sharp dissensions. During the 1940s and 1950s, when neo-evangelical spokespersons had called for an evangelical social program, they had assumed it would be a Christianized version of Republicanism. By the 1960s their movement and a growing number of colleges associated with it were producing a second generation that was calling for more progressive political stances. Vietnam polarized everyone over these issues, and arch-conservatives like J. Howard Pew demanded that evangelicals take unreservedly pronationalist and procapitalist positions. Carl Henry, though solidly Republican, nonetheless lost his job at *Christianity Today,* partly owing to his unwillingness to be sufficiently militant. He was replaced in 1968 by Harold Lindsell, who readily provided Christianized versions of the rhetoric of Spiro Agnew during the Nixon era. This militantly conservative political stance of the evangelical "establishment" sparked a reciprocal action on the left. In 1971 dissident students at Trinity Evangelical Divinity School (a leading center for "establishment evangelicalism") organized The People's Christian Coalition and founded an underground newspaper, *The Post-American,* later becoming *Sojourners,* published by the radical evangelical Sojourner's Community in Washington, D.C. Senator Mark Hatfield became the best-known supporter of this movement. During the 1970s a spectrum of well-represented evangelical political stances emerged. By now there were articulate evangelical groups championing women's equality, pacifism, and progressive versions of social justice.[20] A conservative old guard advocated opposing views. Evangelical social-political involvement, which neo-evangelical leaders had called for in the 1940s and 1950s, now indeed emerged, but as a prime source of division.

At the same time there emerged the closely parallel issue of biblical inerrancy. Although the new evangelicals had attempted to reform fundamentalism, an important group in this "establishment" party had never wanted to break with fundamentalist militancy. "Inerrancy," a real concern in its own right, also symbolized other concerns. Progressive evangelicals usually were relatively sensitive to the importance of historical context for understanding the absolute claims of the gospel. This stance opened the door to more progressive interpretations of the gospel's social implications, and also engendered an openness to nondestructive aspects of higher criticism. Hence, for progressive evangelicals, the "inerrancy" of Scripture usually implied a wooden hermeneutic that tended to interpret the Bible simply as a set of true propositions, without adequately taking into account the original biblical standards of meaning. Conservatives reasoned that inaccuracies in the original Scriptures would be unworthy of God and would undermine biblical authority. Conservatives on this issue were unlikely to have made even modest concessions to the relativizing tendencies of progressive modern thought.[21]

20. These developments are discussed by Richard Quebedeaux, *The Young Evangelicals: Revolution in Orthodoxy* (New York: Harper & Row, 1974) and *The Worldly Evangelicals* (San Francisco: Harper & Row, 1980), and by Robert Booth Fowler, *A New Engagement: Evangelical Political Thought, 1966-1976* (Grand Rapids: Eerdmans, 1983).

21. A partial bibliography of the works debating this issue is provided by Mark A. Noll, "Evangelicals and the Study of the Bible," in Marsden, ed., *Evangelicalism and Modern America,* pp. 198-99.

By the early 1970s, two major evangelical denominations, the Southern Baptist Convention and the Lutheran Church—Missouri Synod, were embroiled in controversies over inerrancy. In 1976 *Christianity Today* editor Harold Lindsell successfully revived inerrancy as a primary issue in transdenominational evangelicalism, suggesting in his much-discussed *The Battle for the Bible* that whoever denied inerrancy was not an evangelical at all.[22]

The transdenominational movement to reform fundamentalism was thus irreparably split over a combination of political and doctrinal issues. "Neo-evangelicals" were so divided among themselves that the term lost its meaning. By the late 1970s, no one, not even Billy Graham, could claim to stand at the center of so divided a coalition.

In addition to these negative forces dividing the movement there were positive ones related to evangelical success. As evangelicalism in the late 1970s reemerged into prominence in American public life, the movement produced spinoffs that shone more brightly than the fragmenting ex-fundamentalism that once provided a sort of center. One of these was the Moral Majority, arising from the unexpected quarter of separatist fundamentalism. Jerry Falwell was in fact a reformer of fundamentalism, whose role in some ways paralleled that of Graham and his new evangelical cohorts of the 1950s. "Neo-fundamentalist" is an appropriate term for Falwell's movement. While holding to the fundamentalist heritage of ecclesiastical separatism (and hence remaining distant from Graham), Falwell tried to bring fundamentalists back toward the centers of American life, especially through political action. Politics meant making alliances. Stricter fundamentalists, like Bob Jones III, condemned Falwell as a pseudofundamentalist. Falwell, nonetheless, proved that the fundamentalist militant "either-or" style suited the political mood of the era. While the evangelical "establishment" was immobilized by internal divi-

22. Harold Lindsell, *The Battle for the Bible* (Grand Rapids: Zondervan, 1976).

sions, Falwell took over the program of its right wing and mobilized many Americans with fundamentalist decisiveness.[23]

The Moral Majority rode the Reagan wave to success, a strategy apparent from their almost uncritical endorsement of the new president's domestic and foreign policies. The Reagan administration, in turn, adopted some of the rhetoric of the religious Right, but it did little substantively (except through court appointments) to promote such leading concerns of the right wing as antiabortion and prayer in public schools.

Although impossible to measure, perhaps evangelicalism's greatest political impact on American policy during the past fifty years has been its role in broadening the popular base for an almost unreserved support for the state of Israel. The Moral Majority only articulated a much more widely held evangelical view on this issue. Dispensationalist teaching, so widespread in the movement since the 1930s, centers on predictions that the state of Israel will play a crucial role in God's plan for the end time. Even most of those neo-evangelicals who abandoned the details of dispensationalism still retained a firm belief in Israel's God-ordained role. This belief is immensely popular in America, though rarely mentioned in proportion to its influence. For instance, during the 1970s the best-selling book in America (though never on the *New York Times* "best-seller" list) was Hal Lindsey's *The Late Great Planet Earth*.[24]

The largest group to hold such prophetic views and, more broadly considered, the largest evangelical force to overwhelm the old fundamentalist reform movement was the

23. A fine discussion of the extensive literature on the fundamentalist Christian right is Richard V. Pierard, "The New Right in American Politics," in Marsden, ed., *Evangelicalism and Modern America*, pp. 161-74. Falwell's differences with stricter fundamentalists are well described in Jerry Falwell, with Ed Dobson and Ed Hindson, *The Fundamentalist Phenomenon: The Resurgence of Conservative Christianity* (Garden City, NY: Doubleday, 1980).

24. Grand Rapids: Zondervan, 1970. Lindsey's work and related views of the Middle East are discussed in Timothy P. Weber, *Living in the Shadow of the Second Coming: American Premillennialism 1875-1982*, enlarged edition (Grand Rapids: Zondervan, 1983).

charismatic movement. By 1979, 19 percent of all Americans identified themselves as charismatic or pentecostal.[25] This phenomenal development on the American religious scene would have seemed bizarre to predict in 1930. One of the manifestations of religious resurgence in the 1950s had been growth of healing revivalism among pentecostal evangelists. An offshoot was the formation, in 1951, of the Full Gospel Business Men's Fellowship International under the leadership of David du Plessis, an Assemblies of God minister and a friend of the leading faith healer, Oral Roberts. Du Plessis worked assiduously and successfully during the next decade to carry the pentecostal message beyond the traditional pentecostal denominations and beyond the poorer economic groups with which it had been largely associated. By the early 1960s charismatic renewal movements had begun in Episcopal, Presbyterian, Lutheran, and other mainline denominations. Soon it reached the Catholic church, where it also found fertile soil. By 1979, 18 percent of all American Catholics were charismatic.[26]

This development fostered a major shift in evangelicalism, substantially bringing to an end hostilities that had still been intense as late as 1960. (The Moral Majority's political alliance with Roman Catholics on "family issues" further promoted this shift.) The spread of the charismatic movement throughout Christendom was due not so much to central leadership, or to prominent personalities, as to effective decentralization. Through small groups and intense communities, the movement grew at seemingly geometrical rates, thus bringing renewal and spreading the gospel at home and abroad.[27] The burgeoning charismatic movement also changed the character of much of evangelicalism in important ways. The emphasis shifted both toward the experiential aspects of Christianity, a sense of closeness to Jesus through the Spirit

25. Richard Quebedeaux, *The New Charismatics*, II (San Francisco: Harper & Row, 1983), 84.
26. Ibid.
27. Ibid., passim.

dwelling within, and toward its therapeutic aspects. The reputed benefits of Christianity for health, success, and personal fulfillment became one of the movement's most common themes.[28] Messages incorporating such emphases were proclaimed by the prominent television evangelists who flourished in the 1970s and 1980s. Among those with the largest ministries, Oral Roberts, Jimmy Swaggart, Jim Bakker of the "PTL Club," and Pat Robertson of the "700 Club" were all charismatic. By 1985 Oral Roberts, for instance, was operating with a budget of close to $2 million dollars per week.[29] In such circumstances the demands of the market were bound to have some impact on the messages preached. By the mid-1980s Pat Robertson was showing himself particularly adept at combining the popular therapeutic emphases of healing pentecostalism with the equally popular political patriotism and conservatism that had won such wide support for (the noncharismatic) Jerry Falwell and the Moral Majority.

Such developments had to be viewed with mixed feelings by the former reformers of fundamentalism who had attempted to build an evangelical coalition around Billy Graham in the 1960s. Evangelicalism was succeeding in remarkable ways. Its most prominent representatives, however, seemed to be moving away from the group that had a plausible claim to embody the core of the transdenominational evangelical tradition that could be traced back through fundamentalism to the days of Moody, Finney, Edwards, and Whitefield. Political fundamentalism picked up one strand that had always been present in that tradition, but ran to what seemed an extreme of self-serving nationalism. The charismatic revival picked up another important strand, namely, concern for individual spirituality, which could be traced back to the Great Awakening. This revival, however, also marked something of a departure

28. James Davison Hunter documents these themes in his *American Evangelicalism: Conservative Religion and the Quandary of Modernity* (New Brunswick, NJ: Rutgers University Press, 1983).

29. David Edwin Harrell, Jr., *Oral Roberts: An American Life* (Bloomington: Indiana University Press, 1985), p. 485.

from the tradition, especially since the message of health and prosperity seemed to intimate that one need not expect to give up the world to follow Christ, but that one would gain the whole world.[30] It can be plausibly argued that evangelicalism's rounding off of the sharp edges of the gospel message between 1960 and 1985 paralleled the gentle modifications of the gospel by Protestant liberalism in the later nineteenth century. Still, many found it difficult to argue with success, which was always at a premium in evangelicalism. People were being converted and brought into churches where most of the essentials of the evangelical message remained unchanged.

During the late 1980s, however, success took it toll, as most of the major television ministries were rocked by scandal, or at least embarrassment. Early in 1987 evangelist Oral Roberts, long known for controversial fund-raising methods, was claiming that God had told him that he would "take him home" unless Roberts's supporters met a current fund-raising goal. While the *Doonesbury* cartoon was making the most of Roberts's tactics, several other evangelists became involved with what seemed a self-caricature. Jim Bakker was accused of sexual improprieties. When Jerry Falwell temporarily took over his PTL ministries he discovered major financial improprieties as well, for which Bakker was eventually convicted. When the sexual scandals first broke, one of Bakker's most outspoken critics was rival evangelist Jimmy Swaggart. Within the year, however, Swaggart was forced by one of his own rivals to admit to his own sexual improprieties and briefly stepped down from his ministry before returning with a new emphasis on forgiveness.

Meanwhile, on the political front Pat Robertson announced his candidacy for the 1988 Republican nomination for the presidency. Under the glare of public scrutiny, Robertson suffered some minor embarrassments for some campaign exaggerations and was ridiculed for his claims of miraculous healing powers

30. A number of the authors in the *Christianity Today* supplement, "Into the Next Century: Trends Facing the Church," 30/1 (January 17, 1986), pp. 1-I to 32-I, express concern over such trends.

and his claim that his prayer had diverted a hurricane from his home base at Virginia Beach. Meanwhile Falwell announced that he was withdrawing from politics and phasing out the Moral Majority. Rather than support the charismatic Robertson who had taken over the Moral Majority agenda, fundamentalist Falwell supported George Bush.

One thing that was clear from all this was that there was little holding evangelicalism together and little to control its extravagances. Organizationally it looked something like the feudal system of the Middle Ages. Leading evangelists built up empires that became focal points of loyalty. In theory all the empires were to be serving the same cause of Christ, but in fact they often were rivals. As became clear in the scandals of the 1980s, the denominations to which evangelists happened to belong had little hold on them, since if threatened with church discipline, the evangelists would simply resign.

One of the striking features of much of evangelicalism is its general disregard for the institutional church. Except at the congregational level, the organized church plays a relatively minor role in the movement. Even the local congregation, while extremely important for fellowship purposes, is often regarded as a convenience to the individual. Ultimately, individuals are sovereign and can join or leave churches as they please. Often they seem as likely to choose a church because it is "friendly" as to do so because of its particular teachings. Denominational loyalties, although still significant for substantial numbers of evangelicals, are incidental for many others, especially those with a transdenominational consciousness who have attempted to bring unity to the movement.

Given this situation, it is remarkable that American evangelicalism has the degree of coherence it does. Little seems to hold it together other than common traditions, a central one of which is the denial of the authority of traditions. Nonetheless, one can attend apparently unconnected evangelical churches at opposite ends of the country and, as likely as not, find nearly identical teachings on most subjects. Probably the principles of the mass market, which emphasize stan-

81

dardization and national campaigns, are primary forces that help maintain this considerable evangelical uniformity.

Whether such centripetal forces for coherence or some countervailing centrifugal forces will prevail is difficult to tell. Perhaps what has been happening over the past two decades is that the traditional transdenominational core has become subordinate to several parties (the charismatic, the conservative-nationalistic political, the progressive evangelical), and that these parties will soon be as distinct as were the mid-twentieth-century fundamentalist and modernist heirs to nineteenth-century evangelicalism. One cannot predict with assurance. Yet, given evangelicalism's typically informal sense of the church, it is difficult to see how any single party could come to dominate and hold the larger movement together. Perhaps it will continue to develop in the form of sympathetic parallel manifestations of related traditions.

One other chief consequence of the lack of an institutional church base, and of the declining role of the traditional denominations, is that evangelicalism's vaunted challenge to the secular culture becomes increasingly difficult to sustain. The movement depends on free enterprise and popular appeal. To some extent conservative churches grow because they promise certainty in times of uncertainty, in the name of the old-time gospel. Yet, with few institutional restraints on what message may legitimately be proclaimed, the laws of the market invite mixes of the gospel with various popular appeals.[31] So the evangelical challenges to the secular "modern mind" are likely to be compromised by the innovative oversimplifications and concessions to the popular spirit of the age. Hence, as is so often the case in church history, the advance of the gospel is bound up with the advance of secularization within the church. Perhaps this conjunction is inevitable in a fallen world. The tares will grow with the wheat.

31. Nathan O. Hatch, "Evangelicalism as a Democratic Movement," in Marsden, ed., *Evangelicalism and Modern America*, pp. 71-82, discusses these dynamics of the movement.

PART TWO

INTERPRETATIONS

3. Evangelical Politics: An American Tradition

M ANY OBSERVERS SEEM to assume that fundamentalist and evangelical entrees into politics are a departure from the American way. In fact, however, for better or for worse, mixes of religion and politics have always been one part of the American political heritage. Perhaps, then, the recent fundamentalist and evangelical political ventures can be best understood as a revival of one of the nation's major political traditions.

In the American colonial era it was assumed that religion and politics went together. Western nations had established churches, and religion was often an integral part of one's national identity. Throughout the colonial era a central political theme was the cold war between the Protestants and Catholics. The British colonies were Protestant outposts in a predominantly Catholic hemisphere. The deep rivalry between Protestants and Catholics dominated American thought in a way not unlike the way the Cold War between Marxist and non-Marxist nations dominated world politics for decades after World War II.

Not only was anti-Catholicism a major foreign policy issue, rivalry between Anglicans and Calvinists was a primary theme in colonial domestic struggles. The heirs to Puritanism

85

in New England and Scotch-Irish Presbyterians in the middle colonies and inland southern settlements were particularly militant in their bitter opposition to the possibility of Anglicanism being imposed as a state-supported religious establishment throughout the colonies. In their purist views, Anglicans were only a step away from Catholicism and tyranny. Baptists had a long-standing heritage of similar views.

In eighteenth-century England dissenters (non-Anglicans) developed a major political tradition around their critique of the privileges of royal and ecclesiastical power. This "Real Whig" outlook drew on the heritage of earlier Puritan opposition to the Anglican crown and formulated principles of liberty and justice that became commonplace among American revolutionaries. These Real Whig principles were articulated in the Enlightenment categories of the day, as being based on self-evident truths of morality. Enlightened Americans, such as Thomas Jefferson, who might be Anglicans by birth, could readily adopt such principles, including their opposition to political establishment of privilege for a particular church.

In the Constitution of 1787 the new nation was defined in secular terms. In part this had to do with antiestablishment sentiments of some of the founders; but just as much it reflected a high regard for religion in American life. As John F. Wilson has suggested, the lack of substantial mention of religion in the Constitution was not because religion was unimportant, but because it was too important. If the Constitution took a stand on the divisive religious issues of the day, its chances of ratification would have been slim.[1] The First Amendment only articulated the hands-off policy toward religion. It ensured both that there would be no federal establishment and that the federal government would not interfere with the free exercise of religion. The intent of the founders was clearly that the federal government would not interfere

1. This point is suggested in John F. Wilson, "Religion, Government, and Power in the New American Nation," in Mark A. Noll, ed., *Religion and American Politics: From the Colonial Period to the 1980s* (New York: Oxford University Press, 1990), pp. 77-91.

even with the state establishment of religion, since in fact such establishments continued in New England for decades after the new nation was founded.

Two traditions of dealing with religion and politics developed out of the American revolutionary experience and the unsettled questions left by the Constitution. On the one hand were those in Jeffersonian tradition who saw religion as tribal and divisive. They noted how ethnic and regional rivalries were heightened by religious conflicts that threatened national unity. Government, then, should best distance itself from direct religious interests. In this tradition acceptance of diversity became a particularly important moral duty. Baptists and other champions of protection of the churches from the state supported such policies.

On the other hand was another tradition, represented most strongly in New England, that saw a more positive role for Christianity in national life. They too feared tribal diversity, but were intent on uniting the nation under divinely sanctioned moral principles. Like their Puritan forebears, they believed the Bible was an important guide for national righteousness. In their reading of the Real Whig tradition they emphasized not disestablishment so much as a mythology that had become important to American republicanism. According to this tradition, religious hierarchy and political authoritarianism went hand in hand. So on one side of the ledger were Catholicism, Anglicanism, centralized monarchical power, corruption, and tyranny; on the other side were Protestantism, Puritanism, representative government, virtue, and freedom. The American way thus had strong religious and ethical dimensions.

Particularly important in the early nineteenth century was an evangelical version of this outlook with a strong New England component and Puritan heritage. The Great Awakening of the eighteenth century had provided a bridge between Puritanism and democratic revolution. The Second Great Awakening, continuing throughout the first half of the century and longer, expanded the cultural influence of revivalist or evangelical Protestantism. Especially in the North, this heritage furnished the religious rationale for the cultural out-look that became one of the long-standing components in the basic patterns of American political life.

Those who adopted this outlook were usually English and religiously evangelical (or sometimes Unitarian). Culturally aggressive New England Yankees provided the leadership for this party. Reflecting the Puritan heritage, they sought the conversion of individuals and also strongly favored applying Christian principles to the transformation of society. This transformation would be accomplished by converted individuals who cultivated virtues of industry, thrift, and personal purity, but also by voluntary societies of such individuals who would band together for religious, educational, and political causes.

One of the early political expressions of this impulse was a phenomenon that, outside of this context, would appear as a total anomaly in American political history, the Anti-Mason party. The secret order of the Masons appeared to these evangelicals as an ominous false religion, one that appealed especially to freethinkers. In 1828 Anti-Masons were numerous enough to deliver nearly half of New York's electoral votes to John Quincy Adams. They soon merged with the new Whig party and became the base for that party's important "conscience" wing, including such strong proponents of antislavery as Thaddeus Stevens and William H. Seward. Evangelist Charles Finney was an ardent anti-Mason. (After the Civil War, when the antislavery issue was settled, Finney returned to the unfinished business of anti-Masonry, allying himself with Jonathan Blanchard, president of Wheaton College in Illinois.)

While the Whig party of the 1830s and 1840s included a substantial New England element, which promoted the effort to regulate society according to evangelical principles,[2] the drive took on a new shape with the demise of the Whig party.

The new factor in the equation was the rise of Catholic

2. Daniel Walker Howe, *The Political Culture of the American Whigs* (Chicago: University of Chicago Press, 1979), provides an excellent discussion of these themes.

political power. Before the mid-nineteenth century the American rivalries had been intra-Protestant. The Scotch-Irish, for instance, were pivotal in American politics through the nation's first half-century. Disliking the New Englanders and New England schemes for moral regulation, they allied themselves with the South, which dominated the politics of the early era. In the 1850s, however, the Catholic threat changed the picture. Catholics who also did not like Yankee ideals of a monolithic Protestant moral commonwealth swelled the ranks of the Democrats. The Scotch-Irish despised the Catholics even more than they disliked the New Englanders and so left the Democratic fold. So did some Baptists and Methodists. As historian Robert Kelley observes, whereas previously the party of culturally aggressive Protestantism had been *English*, now it was a *British* lineup against the detested Irish Catholics.[3]

Explicit anti-Catholicism emerged as the major political issue of the early 1850s. In 1856 the anti-Catholic, nativist Know-Nothing party won 21 percent of the popular vote for its presidential candidate, Millard Fillmore. Then it merged with the antislavery and purely regional Republican party.

The result was that the Republican party had a strong Puritan-evangelical component, bent on regulating the society according to Christian principles. Antislavery was the great achievement of this outlook; but antialcohol and anti-Catholicism were just as much its trademarks.

One thing this party was doing was establishing an insider-versus-outsider mentality toward America and Americanism. Ethnically it was predominantly British; economically it was thoroughly allied with the dominant business community. Both these features reinforced its insider view of itself. The Puritan-Methodist ethic of self-help, moral discipline, and social responsibility dominated much of American education and defined its version of Americanism.

In the meantime, the Democratic party after the 1840s

3. Robert Kelley, *The Cultural Pattern of American Politics* (New York: Knopf, 1979), pp. 278-79.

INTERPRETATIONS

was becoming increasingly the party of outsiders. Its two strongest components were Catholics and Southerners, two groups who had almost nothing in common except their common disdain of Republicanism, with its self-righteous evangelical penchant to impose its version of Christian morality on the whole nation. Northern evangelicals, such as Congregationalists, New School Presbyterians, most Methodists, and most Baptists, usually voted Republican. High Church, liturgical, and confessional Protestants, including some German Lutherans, all of whom had reservations about the evangelical-Puritan version of a Christian America, on the other hand, were more likely to vote Democratic. So were an important group of evangelical Protestants who, in the tradition of Roger Williams, were sufficiently sectarian to question the possibility of ever establishing a Christian political order.[4]

Though the Republican party was a pragmatic coalition and not simply an evangelical voluntary society writ large, a clue to its image of itself as building a Protestant Christian moral consensus is found in the notorious remark by James G. Blaine during the presidential campaign of 1884. The Democrats, he said, were the party of "Rum, Romanism, and Rebellion." On the one hand, it is revealing of the party's Protestant nativist and moral reform heritage that a shrewd politician such as Blaine would make such a remark. On the other hand, since the quip was thought to have cost Blaine the election, it may be taken as signaling the end of the era, begun with the anti-Mason campaigns, when evangelical Protestantism would be an explicitly partisan factor in American political life. Although the symbolic evangelical issue of prohibition remained prominent for another half-century, neither party could afford to be as overtly sectarian as before. The parties were closely enough matched that Republicans had to cultivate

4. Howe, *Political Culture*, pp. 17, 18, 159, 167. A very detailed and sophisticated analysis of these patterns for a later period is offered by Philip R. VanderMeer, *The Hoosier Politician: Officeholding and Political Culture in Indiana: 1896–1920* (Urbana: University of Illinois Press, 1985), pp. 96-120.

some Catholic support and Democrats, some evangelical. This situation was a major change from a period when religion had largely worked against national consensus.

The real turning point to the reorientation of American politics came in 1896, when the Democrats ran the evangelical William Jennings Bryan for president. By the time Bryan had run twice more, in 1900 and 1908, the Democratic party included an interventionist reformist element, much like the Republican party, including even strong sentiments for the archevangelical cause of Prohibition.[5] Democrats ended the progressive era by electing Woodrow Wilson. Though a Southerner, the Presbyterian Wilson was as Puritan as any New Englander who ever held office.

Just as revealing, however, was what was happening to the Republicans in the meantime. The party of McKinley and Mark Hanna had toned down its evangelical image and attracted some Catholic constituency. Nonetheless they were still an overwhelmingly Protestant party with strong assimilationist goals. They represented centripetal forces in America attempting to counter centrifugal tendencies accentuated by immigration. Public education became sacrosanct as one means for teaching immigrants the American way and American virtues. The social gospel was a program for Christianizing America, but without the offense of the old exclusivist gospel of revivalism. In other words, Republicans were still building a Christian consensus, but were suppressing the exclusivist evangelical Protestant elements so as to be able to absorb the new immigrants within their domain.

In effect, the liberal Protestantism and slightly secularized social reform of the progressive era allowed the heirs to accomplish once again what their more explicitly evangelical fathers and mothers had achieved in the 1860s, northern Protestant

5. Paul Kleppner, *Who Voted: The Dynamics of Electoral Turnout, 1870–1980* (New York: Praeger, 1982), pp. 77-78. Cf. Kleppner, "From Ethnoreligious Conflict to 'Social Harmony': Coalitional and Party Transformations in the 1980s," in Seymour Martin Lipset, ed., *Emerging Coalitions in American Politics* (San Francisco: Institute for Contemporary Studies, 1978), pp. 41-59.

dominance. As Robert Kelley puts it, the party patterns set in the progressive era, from 1894 to 1930, coincided with "the years of Northern WASP ascendency in all things, including government, literature, scholarship, the arts, and the economy."[6]

So we see an instance of what Martin Marty long ago pointed out as an American pattern of secularization. Secularization in America took place not by a developing hostility between religion and the dominant culture, but by a blending of their goals. So Republican-Protestant hegemony no longer had to be explicitly Protestant. It just represented a certain concept of civilization. Civilization was equivalent in most minds to Christian civilization. It could be advanced by reforming progressive moral principles that people from all traditions might share. Many Democrats of the era, represented by Bryan and Wilson, adopted this slightly secularized Protestant vision as much as did Republicans. The immense American missionary enthusiasm of this era, sweeping through it colleges, reflected this same impulse to help the world by advancing Christian civilization. Wilson's secularized postmillennial vision of the American mission—to make the world safe for democracy—reflected a similar outlook. Religion, in short, had begun to work toward consensus.

Nonetheless, despite this softening of the Protestant hegemony into a melting-pot ideal of citizenship, democracy, and values taught to all in the public schools, the realignment of 1896 did not entirely disrupt the older party patterns.[7] At least through the election of 1960 the strongest bases for the Democratic party were solid South and Catholic communities. Old-line Protestants still tended to be disproportionately Republican. With the coming of the Depression and the New Deal, however, economic issues dominated party politics. Except when the Democrats ran Catholics in 1928 and 1960, explicit religion was relegated to a ceremonial role.

Although many politicians were Catholics during this era,

6. Kelley, *Cultural Pattern*, p. 285.
7. VanderMeer, *Hoosier Politician*, shows that in general the old patterns held in Indiana during the progressive era.

almost none were Catholic politicians in the substantive sense of elected leaders applying Catholic principles to politics. Rather, Catholic politicians were Americanizing. And the price of being an American politician if you were a Catholic was to leave your substantive Catholicism at the church door. Al Smith summarized the attitude when in response to a question by a reporter about the Pope's latest encyclical he replied, "What in hell is an encyclical?"[8] Catholics had learned to play the twentieth-century game of appealing to the nation's religious heritage, but in a purely ceremonial way. John F. Kennedy was particularly adept at the use of the symbols of American civil religion.[9]

After the progressive era, almost the only place where religion played a substantive role in American politics was in the civil rights movement. Blacks, whose political style had been set by mid-nineteenth-century Republican models and for whom the clergy were traditional community spokespersons in the pattern of Puritan New England, could still challenge the collective conscience of the nation.

The wider pattern, especially from 1896 to about 1968, was a growing ideal of secularized consensus. Despite the persistent ethnoreligious patterns, some differing economic policies, and differing degrees of cold warriorism, the two parties were now much alike. With some significant exceptions, it was difficult to find any difference in principle between them. Rather, the genius of American politics seemed to be that the two parties did not stand for much of anything. George Wallace's campaign slogan of 1968 that there was not "a dime's worth of difference" between the two parties seemed accurate. Supporters of Eugene McCarthy could agree.

Martin Marty has referred to a "four-faith" pluralism that emerged in consensus America of the 1950s. As Will Herberg showed in 1955, although American Protestants, Catholics, and

8. Quoted in James Hennesey, S.J., "Roman Catholics and American Politics, 1900-1960: Altered Circumstances, Continuing Patterns," in Mark A. Noll, ed., *Religion and American Politics*, p. 313.

9. Robert N. Bellah, "Civil Religion in America," *Daedalus* 96 (Winter 1967), 1-5.

Jews had differing formal religions, they had much in common in the operative religion of faith in the American way of life.[10] Marty adds the fourth faith of secularism, acceptable as a private option and still fitting within the consensus.[11]

From our retrospective vantage point, one of the striking things about this accurate portrayal of American public life in the consensus era is the lack of any role for explicitly evangelical Protestantism.

What had happened was that, as mainline Protestants blended into a secularized consensus, fundamentalists, conservative Protestants, or explicit "evangelicals" were forced out. Although during the 1920s they had gained some national prominence in antievolution campaigns and in opposition to Al Smith, they soon faded as a serious political force. Even though, during the next forty years, from 1928 to 1968, there were always right-wing evangelists trying to rally support on political issues, most evangelicals remained on the fringes of American politics. Either they lapsed into political inactivity, or blended in with conservative Republicans in the North or as birthright Democrats in the South. But in this separation, it is important to note, evangelicals were beginning to nurture dissent that would one day threaten the consensus. They dissented first of all against the liberal theology that made the consensus possible, but also against some of the progressive social policies that grew out of the social gospel.

Though no one would have predicted it in 1968, this

10. Will Herberg, *Protestant-Catholic-Jew* (Garden City, NY: Doubleday, 1955).

11. In *The New Shape of American Religion* (New York: Harper & Row, 1958), pp. 76-80. Marty was already talking about America's fourth faith as "secular humanism" (following John Courtney Murray in the usage). He also remarked that "it has an 'established church' in the field of public education." Presumably, discussions such as Murray's and Marty's were behind Justice Hugo Black's famous reference to "secular humanism" as a religion in a 1961 Supreme Court decision. Such sober roots for the term run against claims (as by Sean Wilentz, "God and Man at Lynchburg," *The New Republic*, April 25, 1988, p. 36) of "the invention of secular humanism as a mass religion" by fundamentalists.

94

group soon emerged as a considerable political force. By 1968 the liberal New Deal consensus had broken down. The Vietnam War, the rioting of the blacks, and the counterculture brought down the illusion of a liberal-Protestant-Catholic-Jewish-secular-good citizenship-consensus. While progressives tried to rebuild a more thoroughly secular and more inclusivistic and pluralistic consensus, conservatives sharply disagreed. Capitalizing at first on what seemed a largely secular backlash, as suggested by Vice President Spiro Agnew's popularity in claiming a "silent majority," they mobilized around anticommunism and love-it-or-leave-it Americanism. Then, after the Vietnam War and the presidency of Richard Nixon, a new, more religious coalition began to coalesce around ethical issues such as antiabortion, antipornography, anti-ERA, and symbolic religious issues such as school prayer.

After 1976 it became clear that a substantial evangelical, fundamentalist, and Pentecostal-charismatic constituency could be mobilized around these issues. Only a portion of theologically conservative evangelicals, however, adopted this stance on the political Right. The evangelical movement itself was a divided coalition that at best maintained a tenuous antiliberal theological unity among a myriad of subgroups and denominations. Although a solid contingent of evangelicals could be organized, as in the Moral Majority or in the Pat Robertson campaign, evangelicalism was far from unified as a political force.

What those who did mobilize helped to do, however, was very significant for the patterns of American political life. They helped supply a rhetoric to bring one wing of the Republican party back toward its nineteenth-century heritage. A striking element that was gone, however, was the anti-Catholicism. Evangelicals and conservative Catholics (as well as Mormons and members of the Unification Church) now made common cause on anticommunist and family issues. Such remarkable alliances suggested that, despite the explicitly evangelical stance of the leadership of the religious Right, it also was forming a political consensus in which the exclusiveness of evangelicalism would be toned down. At the same time the religious New Right drew in the natural Anglo-Protestant evangelical constituency of the South, which adopted the renewed Christian America ideal with particular fervor. Though not overtly racist, the new coalition had forsaken its nineteenth-century heritage of advocating the black cause.

As was true for nineteenth-century evangelical Republicans in the era of Ulysses S. Grant, what conservatives actually got in the White House with the victory of Ronald Reagan fell far short of the Christian America of their rhetoric. The mixture of high moral aspirations for Christian civilization with the pragmatic individualistic acquisitiveness of business interests always compromised the ideal. The advent they helped usher in proved to be the second Gilded Age.

Despite these anomalies, which demonstrated that the conscience wing of Republicanism had not actually taken over, an important component of the American political heritage had been revived. Nineteenth-century anti-Masonry and the contemporary war on secular humanism are generically related, even if the center of gravity has moved south. In the face of growing pluralism and moral inclusivism, which became increasingly the trademarks of the Democratic party, one significant wing of Republicanism recovered the ideals of building a coalition around a militant, broadly Christian, antisecularist, and anticommunist heritage. As the end of the twentieth century approaches, this view of the essence of what it means to be an American conflicts sharply with a more inclusivist moral vision.

Robert Wuthnow points out that political conservatives are not the only ones to have a religious-moral vision for the nation. Rather, he observes, America has two civil religions:

> The conservative vision offers divine sanction to America, legitimates its form of government and economy, explains its privileged place in the world and justifies a uniquely American standard of luxury and morality. The liberal vision raises questions about the American way of life, scrutinizes its political and economic policies in the light of transcendent concerns and challenges Americans to

act on behalf of all humanity rather than their own interests alone.[12]

Just as Americans generally are divided concerning these competing moral visions, so are evangelicals divided. Disproportionate numbers of white evangelicals have adopted the conservative exclusivist vision; but the vision more critical of nation and self-interest is an equally venerable part of a heritage that goes back at least to Roger Williams. Likewise strong is a view with roots in the Revolutionary era, which recognizes that America is divided tribally into religious-ethnic groups and that therefore a high moral principle in public life is to keep explicit religion of politics. Jimmy Carter, who held something like this view, was the only practicing evangelical to be president during the 1980s, a simple fact to take into account when considering why most evangelicals did not vote for Pat Robertson. Robertson, Jerry Falwell, and other leaders of the Christian Right do represent the revival of an American political heritage, one that has a long tradition of attempting to set evangelical moral standards for the nation; but even for evangelicals, it is only one of America's religious heritages.

12. Robert Wuthnow, "Divided We Fall: America's Two Civil Religions," *Christian Century,* April 20, 1988, p. 398. Wuthnow's *The Restructuring of American Religion* (Princeton: Princeton University Press, 1988) contains an outstanding discussion of political and religious realignments.

4. Preachers of Paradox: Fundamentalist Politics in Historical Perspective

I F HISTORY HAS LAWS, the first is that it is usually unpre-dictable. Who in the 1950s anticipated the upheavals of the 1960s? Or who in 1970 clearly projected the conservative religious resurgences of the next decade? So when we look at the religious New Right in America today we cannot say whether it marks the dawn of a new spiritual era, a phase in recurrent cycles of social and spiritual anxiety, or the last gasp of an old order. All we can agree on, perhaps, is that theories of secularization that predicted correlations of scientific-technological advance and spiritual decline are in deep trouble.

Such theories themselves combined a violation of history's first law with the biases of secularist scholars. In America such prejudice has been directed particularly against revivalist evangelicalism. During most of this century scholars had difficulty taking this tradition seriously and integrating it into their understandings of the American past. Theory and wish converged to suggest that traditionalist Protestantism would wither in the bright sun of modern culture. During the late nineteenth and early twentieth centuries, secularist intellectuals were locked in a bitter struggle to free themselves from religious control and review. Evangelicalism was the semi-official religion of the old order and had controlled much of academic life. Secularists, when freed from the repressive features of evangelical ideology and mores, completed their revolution by eradicating evangelicalism from academia and public life together. During the first half of the twentieth century the history of the nation was rewritten accordingly. Previously the Protestant roots of the nation had been uncritically lauded and sentimentalized; now they were presented as repressive[1] or, more often, were simply ignored. Evangelical religion was regarded as though it had been peripheral and hence all the more dispensable to American culture. To choose just one example, generations of American students learned of the nineteenth century with no intimation that, as Perry Miller later observed, "the dominant theme in America from 1800 to 1860 is the invincible persistence of the revival technique."[2]

Whereas in the previous chapter we considered evangelical and fundamentalist politics from the perspective of American political history, the purpose of this essay is to understand the religious New Right by looking at it from the perspective of the internal history of evangelicalism and fundamentalism in America. So considered, we find in current fundamentalism the amalgamation of a fascinating variety of traditions. Some are highly intellectualized and some highly emotional, some

---

1. Particularly striking, for example, are some of the harsh treatments of the Puritans. See, for example, Brooks Adams, *The Emancipation of Massachusetts* (Boston: Houghton, Mifflin & Company, 1887), pp. 1-2, 42, and passim; James Truslow Adams, *The Founding of New England* (Boston: Atlantic Monthly Press, 1921), pp. 66, 174, and passim; and Vernon Parrington, *The Colonial Mind, 1620-1800* (New York: Harcourt, Brace & Company, 1927), pp. 5, 15, 29, and passim. The Puritans, safely in the past, were the first religious group to be rehabilitated by secularist scholars, beginning around 1930. R. Stephen Warner, "Theoretical Barriers to the Understanding of Evangelical Christianity," *Sociological Analysis* 40/1 (1979), 1-9, documents the persistence of such biases among sociologists of religion.

2. Perry Miller, *The Life of the Mind in America: From the Revolution to the Civil War* (New York: Harcourt, Brace & World, 1965), p. 7.

elitist-establishmentarian and some directed toward outsiders, some concerned with public policy and some privatistic, and all are mixed with various American assumptions and folklore. During the twentieth century these were fused together, transformed, and sometimes fragmented by intense efforts simultaneously to fight American secularists and to convert them. The result is a movement fraught with paradoxes.

FUNDAMENTALISTS AND EVANGELICALS

As we have seen in earlier chapters, the broad fundamentalist coalition that emerged after World War I included political causes as well as efforts to fight modernism in the churches. William Jennings Bryan's antievolution campaign was the best-known fundamentalist political effort. A number of fundamentalist evangelists, such as Billy Sunday, William B. Riley of Minneapolis, and Frank Norris of Texas laced their messages with political pronouncements, featuring patriotism and Prohibition and attacking Marxism, socialism, evolutionism, and Catholicism.

Though such fundamentalist political efforts continued, the 1930s brought stronger emphases on evangelism and rebuilding. The chief question dividing the movement was whether true Christians ought to separate from unbelief and form their own churches. Should fundamental Christians continue to support denominations that taught un-Christian doctrines and send out missionaries who did not preach the gospel?[3]

Dispensational premillennialism, which continued to spread among fundamentalists during this era, provided an added rationale for separation. According to dispensationalism's scheme of world history, the current dispensation, or

3. This dispute is summarized from the separatist side by Robert Lightner, *New-Evangelicalism* (Findlay, OH: Dunham, 1962), and Charles Woodbridge, *The New Evangelicalism* (Greenville, SC: Bob Jones University Press, 1969). For the nonseparatists, see Ronald H. Nash, *The New Evangelicalism* (Grand Rapids: Zondervan, 1963).

"church age," was marked by the regressive corruption of so-called Christian civilization and the apostasy of its large churches. Only a remnant of true believers would remain pure. The Kingdom of Christ would not be brought in by united Christian effort, as the Social Gospel had promised, but only by the dramatic return of Jesus to set up his millennial kingdom in Jerusalem. Dispensationalism thus suggested that Christian political efforts were largely futile. Believers should give up on the illusion of "Christian civilization." They should separate into pure churches and preach the gospel for the higher cause that eternal souls would be saved for eternity. As evangelists often said of the Social Gospel, why try to clean up the state rooms of the *Titanic* when you know it is doomed?

Not all the heirs to the original fundamentalist coalition, however, adopted dispensational beliefs, and not all dispensationalists followed them to both their separatist and apolitical conclusions. Hence by the 1940s and 1950s it was becoming clear that fundamentalism was dividing into several camps. The major division was, as we have seen, between the broader evangelicals or neo-evangelicals who did not demand separation and stricter fundamentalists who did.

Even among the stricter separatist fundamentalists there were differences of opinion over how much one ought to emphasize politics. Some of the leading evangelists, such as John R. Rice, who later became a mentor to Jerry Falwell, stayed away from most political matters. On the other hand, Carl McIntire, founder in 1941 of the ecclesiastically separatist American Council of Christian Churches, was deeply concerned about politics. During the next thirty years McIntire, widely heard by radio audiences, always kept political issues on one of his front burners. Among his sometimes associates or protégés were Billy James Hargis, Verne Kaub, Fred C. Schwartz, and Edgar C. Bundy, all of whom developed vigorous fundamentalist political organizations of their own.[4]

4. Erling Jorstad, *The Politics of Doomsday: Fundamentalists of the Far Right* (Nashville: Abingdon, 1970).

McIntire's career is illustrative of the development of fundamentalist political interests during this era. Having been forced out of the (Northern) Presbyterian Church in 1936, McIntire maintained a typically fundamentalist central focus on church battles. This was expressed in the American Council, which kept up a barrage of attacks on the ecumenical National Council of Churches and World Council of Churches. McIntire was also avidly anti-Catholic, as late as 1945 stating that the Catholic threat outweighed even that of communism.[5] Such ecclesiastical concerns, however, had strong political overtones, the National Council subverting America by promoting the "social gospel" of New Deal socialism and the Catholics plotting world rule by the Pope. Conspiracy to undermine America at home became the chief theme of such political fundamentalists, and communism became by far their chief concern.[6] McIntire himself thrived on exaggerating the numbers of both his friends and his enemies, constantly portraying himself at the center of a fight to the death between the powers of light and darkness. He and his imitators fit well what Richard Hofstadter characterized in the early 1960s as a "Manichean" mentality.[7] Fundamentalist political concerns may have seemed inconsistent with their world-denying dispensationalism and their condemnations of the social gospel; but, whether in theology or politics, their worldview had the unity of accounting for everything as part of organized forces for good or for evil.

By the early 1960s the work of the various fundamentalist political organizations reached something of a peak as it coincided with that of nonfundamentalist anticommunism that had been growing since the McCarthy era. The impact of funda-

5. James Morris, *The Preachers* (New York: St. Martin's Press, 1973), p. 199.

6. Jorstad, *Politics*, p. 44. Anti-Catholicism was revived during the Kennedy election of 1960, but McIntire repudiated it as a factor when Goldwater's running mate in 1964, William Miller, was a Catholic (ibid., p. 119).

7. Richard Hofstadter, *Anti-Intellectualism in American Life* (New York: Random House, 1962), p. 135.

mentalism on other strains of American anticommunism is difficult to assess, but by this time concerted anticommunist-conspiracy-at-home forces were strong enough to raise strong opposition to the Kennedy administration and to augment the nomination of Barry Goldwater for the presidency in 1964.

Hard-line fundamentalists were not nearly as unified in these political efforts as such accounts might suggest. Leaders such as McIntire were too cantankerous to maintain large coalitions, so fundamentalist efforts were fragmented into various empires. More important, many fundamentalists, while personally very conservative politically, were more consistent with their dispensationalist and separatist principles, seeing communist threats and American declines as signs of the times and keeping away from politics or at least keeping politics from a major role in their ministries. So Jerry Falwell in 1965 was still typical of this apolitical fundamentalism, declaring, "I would find it impossible to stop preaching the pure saving gospel of Jesus Christ, and begin doing anything else—including fighting Communism, or participating in civil-rights reforms."[8]

The cultural crisis of the 1960s eventually proved a boon to fundamentalism as it did to many religious groups. The crisis was, in an important sense, a spiritual crisis. The ideals, the belief system, and the eschatology of the mid-twentieth-century version of liberal culture were proving vacuous. The attacks as expressed first by the counterculture were directed against the ideals of a centralized, liberal, nationalistic, scientific, sociological, service, and consumer culture. The failures of the value system of this technological establishment opened the door to vast varieties of new spiritualities. Religion of almost any sort was accepted on campuses by the early 1970s to an extent that was unthinkable in the late 1950s. In this setting, evangelicalism still did not get the headlines, which were reserved for more bizarre movements. Evangelicals

8. Quoted from a sermon, "Ministers and Marchers," by Frances FitzGerald, "A Disciplined, Charging Army," *The New Yorker*, May 18, 1981, p. 63. Falwell since has repudiated this sermon.

generally, however, had a great advantage over most other spiritual beneficiaries of the upheavals of the 1960s. They had already in place a vast network of institutions, ready to absorb and direct the new enthusiasms.[9] Moreover, evangelicals were also prepared for these new opportunities by their skills in modern techniques of promotion, organization, and communication. The movement had always depended on these for its survival.

The broader evangelical movement, of which fundamentalism was one subtype, benefited from the upheavals of the 1960s in paradoxical ways.[10] On the one hand, it capitalized on the decline in prestige of the liberal-scientific-secular establishment, a value system that evangelicals had already proclaimed as illusory and doomed. The decentralizing emphases of counterculture readily could be appropriated to evangelicalism, which already was a hodgepodge of *ad hoc* structures. More important, the people-community impulses of the era were readily translated by evangelicals into personal contacts and small-group meetings, such as groups for Bible study and prayer, that contributed substantially to evangelical growth during the 1970s.

On the other side of the paradox, evangelicalism gained from the deep reactions against counterculture ideals. The instinctive impulses of much of the evangelical constituency were of the Spiro Agnew variety. Translated into spiritual terms, what they saw first in the protests of the young was a more virulent sort of Godless secularism and lawlessness. To many conservative evangelicals such vices were extensions of the permissiveness of the New Deal liberal culture rather than protests against it. Such impressions were indeed reinforced by liberalization of the laws in the direction of permissiveness, such as toward homo-

9. This point is suggested in Jeremy Rifkin, with Ted Howard, *The Emerging Order: God in the Age of Scarcity* (New York: G. P. Putnam's Sons, 1979), p. 104.

10. David Martin, "Revived Dogma and New Cult," in Mary Douglas and Steven Tipton, eds., *Religion and America: Spirituality in a Secular Age* (Boston: Beacon Press, 1983), makes a similar point.

sexuals or abortion, and enforced secularization of schools and public places. During the Vietnam era, however, attacks on the nation and on authority commanded the most attention, so many evangelicals defended with fierce patriotism the nation that they nonetheless regarded as disastrously corrupt.[11]

Evangelicals also benefited from the uncertainties of the Vietnam era and its aftermath by offering decisive answers. The fundamentalist militancy in the heritage encouraged polarized thinking. The metaphors of warfare that dominated that movement suggested that battle lines could be clearly drawn on almost any issue. Confronted with the crisis in authority in a changing and pluralistic society, evangelicals could point to the sure certainty of the word of God. The "inerrancy" of the Bible became an increasingly important symbolic test of faith for much of the movement.[12] Evangelicals generally could draw on the immense residual prestige of the Bible in America as a firm rock in a time of change.[13]

These circumstances—a deeply rooted ideological-spiritual heritage, vigorous institutions, skills in promotion, and an era when people were open to spiritual answers to national and personal crises—combined for the evangelical resurgence of the 1970s. Jimmy Carter's presidency was an appropriate symbol of the new status of the movement, which was growing in fact but also growing much faster in media attention. Carter-as-evangelical suggests some of the variety within evangelicalism at a time when forty or fifty million constituents were attributed to the movement. Carter was a

11. See, for example, the chapter "The Bible Fundamentalist is A GOOD CHRISTIAN CITIZEN," in John R. Rice, *I Am a Fundamentalist* (Murfreesboro, TN: Sword of the Lord Publishers, 1975), pp. 151-79. Rice, editor of *Sword of the Lord,* with a circulation of about 250,000, was not heavily political but adamantly for law and order.

12. A leading signal in the revival of this issue was the publication of Harold Lindsell's *The Battle for the Bible* (Grand Rapids: Zondervan, 1976). By 1980, 100,000 were in print.

13. On the role of the Bible in the evangelical tradition and in American culture see Nathan O. Hatch and Mark A. Noll, eds., *The Bible in America: Essays in Cultural History* (New York: Oxford University Press, 1982).

Southern Baptist and was outside of the movements that claimed to speak for evangelicalism generally. His political stance, moreover, illustrated that one did not have to be politically conservative to be a full-fledged "evangelical." By now the movement had vigorous wings that tended toward liberal democratic politics and a significant, more radical, Anabaptist political voice.[14] Political conservatism, however, was no doubt the most widespread inclination.

The Moral Majority arose in this situation in 1979, capitalizing on the unfocused but conservative political sentiments of many evangelicals and some others. From the viewpoint of the history of evangelicalism, a striking feature of the Moral Majority was that its leadership proudly called itself "fundamentalist." Up to this time the hard-line fundamentalists might have seemed unlikely candidates for exercising national leadership on a large scale. Having split from the larger body of evangelicals, their avowed separatism seemed sufficiently extreme to make any widespread cooperation, even among themselves, appear unlikely.[15] Those who dealt with politics tended to do so in several ways, although these were not mutually exclusive. They might, like Carl McIntire or Billy James Hargis, continue to beat the drums of simplistic anticommunist crusades that dated back to the McCarthy era. All the nation's problems were reduced to communist infiltration of the nation's liberal ecclesiastical, political, and intellectual establishments. Such views attracted a numerically solid but limited constituency. Second, consistent with a long revivalist tradition, fundamentalists occasionally organized in moral campaigns, such as to clean up

14. These movements are studied in Robert Booth Fowler, *A New Engagement: Christian Evangelical Political Thought, 1966-1976* (Grand Rapids: Eerdmans, 1982). They are also covered, sometimes more impressionistically, in Richard Quebedeaux, *The Worldly Evangelicals* (New York: Harper & Row, 1978).

15. George W. Dollar, *A History of Fundamentalism in America* (Greenville, SC: Bob Jones University Press, 1973), p. 248, estimated the total number of separatist fundamentalists at about four million.

textbooks or to fight pornography. Third, like the early Jerry Falwell, many fundamentalists tended to view politics primarily as signs of the times that pointed toward the early return of Jesus to set up a political kingdom in the land of Israel. The sorry moral state of the nation was seen primarily as an impetus for repentance. The new Jerry Falwell and the Moral Majority mobilized not so much the political impulse that had been distinctive to fundamentalism but rather the moral-political impulse that had been one part of the revivalist tradition more generally. Although Falwell came from a fundamentalist background and was pastor of a fundamentalist church, his national moral crusade involved too broad an alliance with "Mormons, Jews, Roman Catholics, Adventists, apostates, New Evangelicals"[16] to suit the strict fundamentalists. Falwell in their view was a "pseudofundamentalist" or, worse, a "neo-evangelical" in disguise.[17] In this dispute, the stricter fundamentalists were probably correct that Falwell's movement was similar to the neo-evangelical movement of the 1940s and 1950s. He was, as Frances Fitz-Gerald has observed,[18] torn between doctrines that demand separation and ambitions for acceptance and influence that demanded compromise. While condemning in good fundamentalist fashion the compromises of Billy Graham, Falwell was moving in the same direction away from strict fundamentalism as did Graham.

In terms of the history of American evangelicalism, Falwell and the Moral Majority perhaps can best be seen as a recombina-

16. "The Moral Majority: An Assessment of a Movement," by James E. Singleton, ca. 1981, p. 16. Cf. "The Fundamentalist Phenomenon or Fundamentalist Betrayal," compiled and edited by James E. Singleton, ca. 1981. These pamphlets are produced by persons sympathetic to Bob Jones University.

17. Jerry Falwell, with Ed Dobson and Ed Hindson, eds., *The Fundamentalist Phenomenon: The Resurgence of Conservative Christianity* (Garden City, NY: Doubleday, 1981), pp. 160-63.

18. "A Disciplined, Charging Army," p. 103. FitzGerald sees this same tension in Falwell's people, who aspire both to separation from the world and to worldly success.

tion of some elements drawn from the neo-evangelical and fundamentalist heritages since 1950. From neo-evangelicalism comes the conception of "secular humanism" as virtually a religious force threatening to displace Christianity entirely from the culture. This critique was articulated around midcentury by a number of neo-evangelical theologians and philosophers who spelled out the incompatibilities of the worldviews derived from Christian presuppositions drawn from Scripture and worldviews founded on atheistic-naturalistic assumptions.[19] Following in a general way the sophisticated suggestions of the Dutch theologian-politician Abraham Kuyper (1837-1920), the neo-evangelicals viewed Western culture as locked in a struggle between these contending worldviews. By the 1970s such ideas in simplified form had filtered to some fundamentalist leaders through, for instance, the immensely popular film series *How Then Should We Live?* (1976) by evangelicalism's well-known quasi-philosopher and evangelist Francis Schaeffer.[20] The fundamentalists further transformed these ideas by putting them into the characteristic fundamentalist paradigm of a simple warfare between the forces of light and darkness. Just as typical of fundamentalist thought, the struggle between contending ideals was personalized as a carefully orchestrated conspiracy. So in the view of Moral Majority spokesman Tim LaHaye, humanists (whom he defines as everyone but Bible believers) have been

19. These themes are developed, for instance, in Carl F. H. Henry, *Remaking the Modern Mind* (Grand Rapids: Eerdmans, 1946), and Edward J. Carnell, *Introduction to Christian Apologetics* (Grand Rapids: Eerdmans, 1948). Some mainstream religious writers developed similar themes and perhaps coined the term "secular humanism" in the 1950s. See Chapter 3, note 11 above.
20. Tim LaHaye, *The Battle for the Mind* (Old Tappan, NJ: Revell, 1980), cites Schaeffer extensively. Falwell, in turn, cites LaHaye for his definition of *humanism*, in *Fundamentalist Phenomenon*, p. 199. The critique of "humanism" and "secular humanism" is not prominent in earlier fundamentalist literature, but does appear especially in connection with non-Christian influences in public schools. For instance, opponents of teaching evolution typically have argued in court cases that it was part of a humanistic religion.

"planted" in strategic places in the United Nations, they teach children in public schools "to read the words *scientific humanism* as soon as they are old enough to read," and 275,000 humanists control American government, education, and media.[21]

The "secular humanist" idea revitalized fundamentalist conspiracy theory. Fundamentalists always had been alarmed at moral decline within America but often had been vague as to whom, other than the Devil, to blame. The "secular humanist" thesis gave this central concern a clearer focus that was more plausible and of wider appeal than the old mono-causal communist-conspiracy accounts. Communism and socialism could, of course, be fit right into the humanist picture; but so could all the moral and legal changes at home without implausible scenarios of Russian agents infiltrating American schools, government, reform movements, and mainline churches. As many analysts of modern society have observed, secular humanism *is* an ideology with a quasi-religious character and involves a number of naturalistic beliefs to give it a rough-hewn unity.[22] The fundamentalists' simplified version of this observation, while extreme, nonetheless pointed to a real secularizing trend in a large area of the culture, so that their claims carried more force of plausible evidence than did most conspiracy theories.

THE PARADOXES OF THE FUNDAMENTALIST NEW RIGHT

The first thing to notice in considering the New Right in light of this fundamentalist and evangelical history is the diversity of the religious movement and hence its sometimes self-contradictory stances toward culture. Fundamentalism

---

21. LaHaye, *Battle*, pp. 27, 74, 97, and 179.
22. For example, cf. Peter L. Berger, "From the Crisis of Religion to the Crisis of Secularity," in Mary Douglas and Steven M. Tipton, eds., *Religion and America: Spirituality in a Secular Age* (Boston: Beacon Press, 1983), pp. 14-24.

from the outset was both a distinct movement or impulse and a coalition of a number of movements. Nineteenth-century American evangelicalism, from which fundamentalism grew, was itself a coalition of several denominational traditions. Similarly, today we can identify at least fourteen varieties of evangelicalism.[23] While these evangelicals share many doctrines, their diversities in inherited stances toward culture and politics are especially pronounced. So on the issues of culture and politics generalizations about evangelicalism are particularly hazardous.

Central to the fundamentalist heritage is a basic tension between positive revivalism and polemics. Fundamentalism developed largely within the revivalist tradition, in which the highest goal was to win other souls to Christ. Controversy could aid revivalism for a time, but in the long run too much controversy and too much cantankerousness could hinder evangelistic efforts. This was one of the issues that divided neo-evangelicals from hard-line fundamentalists after 1940. Fundamentalist separatism, insistence on strict doctrinal purity, and incivility toward persons with other beliefs seemed to the new evangelicals to hinder the spread of the gospel. The evangelism of Billy Graham well represented their impulse. Despite his traditionalist message and his efforts to change individuals, Graham was willing to live with American pluralism. Hard-line fundamentalists were unwilling to accept such compromise of strict separatism. The price of such polemics was that they remained on the fringe where fewer people would take their message seriously.

The tensions between positive revivalism and controversialism are complicated by a second tension that pulls evangelicalism simultaneously in two directions. Simply put, this is a tension between being and not being politically and culturally

---

23. Robert E. Webber, *Common Roots: A Call to Evangelical Maturity* (Grand Rapids: Zondervan, 1978), p. 32. Cullen Murphy, "Protestantism and the Evangelicals," *The Wilson Quarterly,* Autumn 1981, pp. 105-17, identifies twelve varieties.

oriented. This division cuts differently than does the positive revivalist versus polemicist division. Some evangelicals with political-cultural concerns are militant controversialists (fundamentalists), and others are not. Moreover, many evangelicals who stress positive revival also have political-cultural programs, but many others do not. So these two types of tensions produce four combinations of basic ideal types (positive-nonpolitical, positive-political, polemicist-nonpolitical, and polemicist-political).[24]

The tension between emphasizing political-cultural implications of the gospel and eschewing them is also deeply rooted. It is inherent in Christianity itself, which always has wavered between Old Testament and New and between redeeming the city of the world and thinking of the City of God as wholly spiritual or otherworldly. Such ambivalence is particularly strong in American evangelicalism. This is so both because American evangelicalism and fundamentalism fuse so many traditions and because in America itself evangelicals have been cast in vastly different roles in different eras.

The most immediate heritage of fundamentalists comes from their twentieth-century experiences of being a beleaguered and ridiculed minority. Sin and secularism had run rampant over some key parts of American culture. Like twentieth-century sociologists, most fundamentalists believed in laws that declared that the process of secularization was irreversible. In the fundamentalists' case these laws were drawn from dispensational premillennialism, which posited the steady decline of the modern era in preparation for a final world calamity resolved only by the personal return of Christ with avenging armies. Fundamentalists in this worldview were outsiders.[25] They were out-

24. A more refined version of this sort of categorization is found in Richard J. Mouw, "The Bible in Twentieth-Century Protestantism: A Preliminary Taxonomy," in Hatch and Noll, *Bible in America*, pp. 139-62.

25. R. Laurence Moore, "Insiders and Outsiders in American Historical Narrative and American History," *American Historical Review* 87/2 (April 1982), 390-412, provides a helpful account of this outsider theme and its inherent ambiguities.

siders from the power centers of society, its politics, and its cultural life; they viewed themselves as separated from the worldly powers. This separation was indeed selective, not precluding full participation in the nation's economic life and usually not thwarting impulses to patriotism. Some fundamentalists stood as lonely prophets warning of the destruction that was to come and that could be seen in the growing strength of demonic world forces such as Catholicism or communism. More typically, however, fundamentalists and many other evangelicals, sensing themselves to be essentially outsiders, drew on those considerable strands in their revivalist and New Testament heritage that forsook political and cultural aspirations.

If one looks a little further back, however, one finds an almost opposite strand in the heritage. Throughout the nineteenth century, revivalist evangelicalism was the dominant religious force in America, strong enough to be a virtual establishment in this most religious of modern nations. Though often submerged, the images of this historical tradition retained a residual power through the hard days of the twentieth century. When in eras such as the early 1920s or 1980s when the nation was in the midst of a conservative reaction and unfocused anxiety, this establishmentarian side of the tradition could be readily revived.

This political-cultural side of the heritage reflects not at all the premillennialism that was taught in twentieth-century fundamentalism but rather a residual postmillennialism that had dominated nineteenth-century evangelicalism. In this view America has a special place in God's plans and will be the center for a great spiritual and moral reform that will lead to a golden age or "millennium" of Christian civilization. Moral reform accordingly is crucial for hastening this spiritual millennium. Fundamentalists today reject postmillennialism as such, but generically postmillennial ideals continue to be a formidable force in their thinking. Such ideals now appear not so much as Christian doctrine but as a mixture of piety and powerful American folklore. This folklore is a popularization of a version of the Whig view of history, in which true religion

112

and liberty are always pitted against religion and tyranny. America, in this view, was founded on Christian principles embodied in the Constitution and has been chosen by God to be a beacon of right religion and liberty for the whole world.[26]

Puritanism is another powerful source of fundamentalist cultural views. Almost always, Puritan social doctrines are mixed with the Whig version of American history and folklore. One clue to the Puritan connection is the constant use of the jeremiad form. The light of true religion and liberty has dimmed, though only rather recently—sometime since the end of World War II.[27] Up to that time "America has been great because her people have been good," as Jerry Falwell put it.[28] Her moral decline coincided with her international humiliations of the 1970s. These were, in fact, simply cause and effect. While the connections might not seem apparent to human wisdom, we can be sure that God is punishing America for her depravity, an idea inherited directly from the Puritan covenantal tradition. God's blessings and curses are, in Old Testament fashion, contingent on national righteousness or sinfulness. Falwell constantly repeated this theme, suggesting, for instance, that the spread of pornography was causally related, through God's providential control, to national distresses such as the oil crisis.[29] "Our nation's internal problems," he said, characteristically, "are direct results of her spiritual condition."[30]

26. Ronald A. Wells, "Francis Schaeffer's Jeremiad: A Review Article," *The Reformed Journal* 32/5 (May 1982), 16-20, suggests the combination of Whig history and the jeremiad.

27. For example, John R. Price, *America at the Crossroads: Repentance or Repression?* (Indianapolis: Christian House Publishing Company, 1976), pp. 3-7. Cf. Jerry Falwell, *Listen America!* (Garden City, NY: Doubleday, 1980), and LaHaye, *Battle*, passim.

28. Falwell, *Listen America!*, p. 243.

29. Jerry Falwell, interview, *Eternity*, July-August 1980, p. 19.

30. Falwell, *Listen America!*, p. 243. Cf. Price, *America at the Crossroads*, pp. 109-58 and passim, who details at length the covenant parallels between modern America and Old Testament Israel. Also cf. the ideas of Bill Bright, president of Campus Crusade, who at least for a time advocated evangelical political action based on covenantal principles of God's

The continuing strength of this combination of Whig and Puritan views in the religious outlook suggests that it is misleading to characterize the fundamentalist-evangelical heritage as generally "private."[31] One important strand of the revivalist heritage, drawn from pietism, Methodism, and Baptist zeal for separation of church and state, has tended to eschew identifications of the Kingdom of God with social-political programs. Evangelicalism has always been divided within itself on this point, however. During the nineteenth century the Puritan heritage was still a formidable force in shaping evangelicals' quasi-Calvinist visions of a Christian America. Such Puritan culture-dominating ideals persist in the Moral Majority today. Much of evangelicalism accordingly has been of two minds on the question of personal versus social applications of the gospel. Even the Methodist-holiness tradition, certainly a center for some strongly privatistic impulses, has sometimes supported postmillennial visions of social reform. Fundamentalism has sometimes resolved its internal dilemma on this point by making distinctions between public "moral" questions that it supports as opposed to illicit mixing of "politics" with religion by liberal church leaders. [32]

A related point is worth noting: Fundamentalists are reputedly highly individualistic. Indeed, fundamentalists are individualistic in the sense of advocating classical liberal economics and in emphasizing the necessity of an individual's personal relation to Jesus. Moreover, their view of the church is nomi-

judgments or blessings. See John A. Lapp, "The Evangelical Factor in American Politics," in C. Norman Kraus, ed., *Evangelicalism and Anabaptism* (Scottdale, PA: Herald Press, 1979), pp. 91-94.

31. The identification of evangelicalism and revivalism as "private" in contrast to "public" Protestantism has been widely promoted by one of the most consistently astute interpreters of American religion, Martin Marty. See, for example, his *Righteous Empire: The Protestant Experience in America* (New York: Harper Torchbooks, 1970).

32. Carl McIntire, for instance, characteristically responded to accusations that he had made the gospel too political with statements such as "What men call politics, to me is standing up for righteousness." Morris, *Preachers*, p. 190.

nalistic; they see it essentially as a collection of individuals. Early in this century theological liberals who were building the Social Gospel movement were quick to point out such individualistic traits and to contrast them with their own more communal emphases. Ever since, this individualistic-privatistic image has dominated views of fundamentalism. Despite the substantial truth to this characterization, there is another side. In fact fundamental churches and national organizations are some of the most cohesive nonethnic communities in America.[33] Certainly the fundamentalist churches offer far stronger community for their members than do their moderate-liberal Protestant counterparts. Moreover, despite the profession of individuality, fundamentalist churches and organizations tend to be highly authoritarian, typically under the control of one strong leader. Although fundamentalist preaching sometimes stresses making up one's own mind, in fact the movement displays some remarkable uniformities in details of doctrine and practice that suggest anything but real individualism in thought.

Returning to the persistence of the quasi-Calvinist vision of cultural dominance, we can see yet another paradox within fundamentalism. Fundamentalism usually has been regarded as essentially anti-intellectual. Again, there is some truth to this accusation. A considerable tradition within American revivalism has always viewed higher education with suspicion.[34] Early Methodists, many Baptists, and other American groups considered an educated clergy a stumbling block to true spirituality. Today some fundamentalist groups insist that education

33. Lowell D. Streiker and Gerald S. Strober, *Religion and the New Majority: Billy Graham, Middle America, and the Politics of the '70s* (New York: Association Press, 1972), pp. 139-40. Most fundamentalists are of northern European descent, but the unity of their communities is not usually based on more narrow ethnic ties.

34. According to the 1978-79 Gallup–*Christianity Today* survey, evangelicals (who include many persons from the rural South) are the least educated of the groups surveyed. Only 9 percent completed university education, while 37 percent had not completed high school. Hunter, "Contemporary Evangelicalism," pp. 123-24.

beyond high school be confined to their own Bible schools. Moreover, bitter opposition to the American intellectual establishment and accusations that too much learning has corrupted liberal and neo-evangelical Protestants are commonplace.

Nonetheless, as we have seen, fundamentalism also reflects the persistence of the Puritan heritage in the American Protestant psyche. This heritage includes a cultural vision of all things, including learning, brought into the service of the sovereign God. Fundamentalists accordingly retain vestiges of this ideal. Schools, including colleges and "universities," are central parts of their empires. Although they may only rarely attain excellence in learning, they seek it in principle and sometimes do attain it. No group is more eager to brandish honorary degrees. Perhaps more to the point, genuine degrees are more than welcome when in the service of the Lord. Nowhere is this clearer than in the creation-science movement, a predominantly fundamentalist effort. While decrying the scientific establishment and people who blindly follow the lead of "experts," the Creation Research Society emphasizes the hundreds of Ph.D.'s who make up its membership.

Even more centrally, fundamentalists are among those contemporary Americans who take ideas most seriously. In this respect they reflect, even if in a dim mirror, the Puritan heritage. For the fundamentalist, what one believes is of the utmost importance. They are, as Samuel S. Hill, Jr., observes, more "truth-oriented" than most evangelical groups.[35] The American intellectual establishment, in contrast, has a tendency to reduce beliefs to something else, hence devaluing the importance of ideas as such. So, for instance, fundamentalist ideas themselves have long been presented as though they were "really" expressions of some social or class interest. It seems fair to inquire in such cases as to who is really the anti-intellectual. To reduce beliefs to their social functions is

35. Samuel S. Hill, Jr., "Popular Southern Piety," in David Edwin Harrell, Jr., ed., *Varieties of Southern Evangelicalism* (Macon, GA: Mercer University Press, 1981), p. 100.

to overemphasize a partial truth and so to underestimate the powers of the belief itself. Consider, for instance, the important fundamentalist belief that God relates to the nation covenantally, rewarding or punishing it proportionately to its moral record. This is a belief, deeply held on religious grounds, about some causal connections in the universe. Throughout the history of America this conception about causality has survived through a number of revolutionary changes in the class and status of its adherents. While, as suggested earlier, social and cultural circumstances strongly influence the expressions of this belief, there is no doubt that the belief itself is sometimes a powerful force in determining the way people behave.

Fundamentalist thought often appears anti-intellectual because of its proneness to oversimplification. The universe is divided in two—the moral and the immoral, the forces of light and darkness. This polarized thinking reflects a crass popularizing that indeed is subversive to serious intellectual inquiry. The fundamentalist worldview starts with the premise that the world is divided between the forces of God and of Satan and sorts out evidence to fit that paradigm. Nevertheless, fundamentalist thinking also reflects a modern intellectual tradition that dates largely from the Enlightenment. Fundamentalist thought had close links with the Baconian and Common Sense assumptions of the early modern era. Humans are capable of positive knowledge based on sure foundations. If rationally classified, such knowledge can yield a great deal of certainty. Combined with biblicism, such a view of knowledge leads to supreme confidence on religious questions.[36] Despite the conspicuous subjectivism

36. Charles W. Allen documents this tendency in southern Baptist fundamentalist Paige Patterson, who says of liberal views: "The Subjectivism of their epistemology reduced easily to a formula, $T = P - C$, i.e., Truth = my Perception minus Certainty. I for one cannot build faith on such a quivering foundation." Quoted from Patterson, "Inerrancy—and the Passover," *The Shopbar* 4 (May 1980), A-1, in Allen, "Paige Patterson: Contender for Baptist Sectarianism," *Review and Expositor* 79/1 (Winter 1982), 110.

throughout evangelicalism[37] and within fundamentalism itself, one side of the fundamentalist mentality is committed to inductive rationalism. More of this in the subsequent chapters.

This commonsense inductive aspect of fundamentalist thinking, rather than being anti-intellectual, reflects an intellectual tradition alien to most modern academics. What is most lacking is the contemporary sense of historical development, a Heraclitean sense that all is change. This contemporary conception of history invites relativism or at least the seeing of ambiguities. Fundamentalists have the confidence of Enlightenment philosophies that an objective look at "the facts" will lead to the truth.[38] Their attacks on evolutionism reflect their awareness that the developmentalist, historicist, and culturalist assumptions of modern thought undermine the certainties of knowledge. Correspondingly, persons attracted to authoritarian views of the Bible are often also attracted to the pre-Darwinian, ahistorical, philosophical assumptions that seem to provide high yields of certainty.

It is incorrect, then, to think of fundamentalist thought as essentially premodern.[39] Its views of God's revelation, for example, although drawn from the Bible, are a long way from the modes of thought of the ancient Hebrews. For instance, fundamentalists' intense insistence on the "inerrancy" of the Bible in scientific and historical detail is related to this modern style of thinking. Although the idea that Scripture does not

37. James Davison Hunter, "Subjectivism and the New Evangelical Theodicy," *Journal for the Scientific Study of Religion* 20/1 (1982), 39-47, documents the subjectivist side of evangelicalism.

38. For example, the apologetics of Josh McDowell, *Evidence that Demands a Verdict: Historical Evidences for the Christian Faith* (San Bernadino, CA: Campus Crusade, 1972). Such objectivist apologetics were dominant in nineteenth-century American evangelicalism.

39. Martin E. Marty makes some valuable comments on this theme in "The Revival of Evangelicalism and Southern Religion," in Harrell, *Varieties of Southern Evangelicalism*, pp. 7-22. Among other things, Marty observes that evangelicals' modernity is reflected in their emphasis on *choice*. Here is another paradox, since evangelicals speak much about both choice and absolute authority.

err is an old one, fundamentalists accentuate it partly because they often view the Bible virtually as though it were a scientific treatise. For example, southern Baptist fundamentalist Paige Patterson remarks: "Space scientists tell us that minute error in the mathematical calculations for a moon shot can result in a total failure of the rocket to hit the moon. A slightly altered doctrine of salvation can cause a person to miss Heaven also."[40] To the fundamentalist the Bible is essentially a collection of true and precise propositions. Such approaches may not be typical of most twentieth-century thought, but they are more nearly early modern than premodern.

Fundamentalist thought is in fact highly suited to one strand of contemporary culture—the technological strand. Unlike theoretical science or social science, where questions of the supernatural raise basic issues about the presuppositions of the enterprise, technological thinking does not wrestle with such theoretical principles. Truth is a matter of true and precise propositions that, when properly classified and organized, will work. Fundamentalism fits this mentality because it is a form of Christianity with no loose ends, ambiguities, or historical developments. Everything fits neatly into a system. It is revealing, for instance, that many of the leaders of the creation-science movement are in applied sciences or engineering.[41]

Fundamentalists in more general ways have proved themselves masters of modern technique. The skillful use of organizational mass mailing and media techniques by the fundamentalist New Right during the 1980s elections similarly demonstrated this mastery of an aspect of modern culture. Such expertise in rationalized technique should hardly be surprising in a Protestant American tradition. Moreover, evangelicalism has long depended for support on effectively mobilizing masses of potential constituents. Evangelist Charles Finney in the early nineteenth century

40. Patterson, *Living in the Hope of Eternal Life* (Grand Rapids: Zondervan, 1968), p. 26, quoted in Allen, "Paige Patterson," p. 110.

41. Dorothy Nelkin, *Science Textbook Controversies and the Politics of Equal Time* (Cambridge: MIT Press, 1977), p. 72.

was in fact one of the pioneers in rationalized techniques of modern advertising and promotion.

The fundamentalist message is also peculiarly suited for large segments of society in the technological age. Fundamentalists have been particularly adept at handling mass communication. If there is a rule of mass communications that the larger the audience the simpler the message must be, fundamentalists and similar evangelicals came to the technological age well prepared. Television ministries flourish best when they provide answers in simple polarities. By contrast, one could hardly imagine a widely popular neo-orthodox television ministry; subtleties and ambiguities would kill it immediately.[42] Such aptness of the message to the age is not confined to TV. Although not often acknowledged by the controllers of public opinion, evangelicals have also dominated the actual best-seller statistics during recent decades.[43] The key to such success is again a simple message. Such simplicity itself bears a paradoxical relationship to contemporary life. On the one hand, it is a reaction against the tensions, uncertainties, and ambiguities that surround modern life and always shape the human condition. At the same time, the ancient simplicities have been given a contemporary shape by the same forces that produce the efficient production and sales of, let's say, McDonald's hamburgers. As the Cathedral at Chartres symbolized the essence of the medieval era, so perhaps McDonald's golden arches may symbolize ours. For better or worse, fundamentalism is a version of Christianity matched to its age.

*   *   *

Fundamentalism, then, is fraught with paradoxes. It is torn between uncivil controversialism and the accepting attitudes

42. This point is suggested in Falwell, *The Fundamentalist Phenomenon*, p. 172, regarding the media advantage of fundamentalists versus "left-wing Evangelicalism."

43. Rifkin and Howard, *Emerging Order*, p. 112.

necessary for being influential and evangelizing effectively. Often it is otherworldly and privatistic; yet it retains intense patriotism and interest in the moral-political welfare of the nation. It is individualistic, yet produces strong communities. It is in some ways anti-intellectual, but stresses right thinking and true education. It accentuates the revivalists' appeal to the subjective, yet often it is rationalistic-inductivist in its epistemology. It is Christianity derived from an ancient book, yet shaped also by the technological age. It is antimodernist, but in some respects strikingly modern. Perhaps most ironically, it offers simple answers phrased as clear polarities; yet it is such a complex combination of traditions and beliefs that it is filled with more ambiguity and paradox than most of its proponents, or its opponents, realize.

5. The Evangelical Love Affair with Enlightenment Science

ONE SCIENCE OR TWO?

IN 1902, Princeton Theological Seminary's Benjamin B. Warfield, who was supposed to be writing an introduction to a volume on apologetics by Francis R. Beattie, a fellow American Presbyterian, made a few perfunctory remarks about Beattie and then quite gratuitously turned to a critique of another conservative Reformed theologian, Dr. Abraham Kuyper of the Netherlands. Warfield, a hard-hitting and sometimes brilliant polemicist in a day of increasingly polite theology, had by this time established his reputation, for better or worse, as the John L. Sullivan of the theological world. He was always ready to spar, even with a close theological ally such as Kuyper. Kuyper was a truly remarkable figure. In addition to being a first-rate theologian, he was a newspaper editor, the founder of a university, the organizer of a denomination, and ultimately prime minister of the Netherlands.

Despite his admiration for Kuyper, Warfield found the Dutch theologian's view of science (and hence his view of Christian apologetics) "a standing matter of surprise." Kuyper denied that there was one unified science for the human race. Rather,

he argued that because there are "two kinds of people," regenerate and unregenerate, there are "two kinds of sciences."
The differences in the two sciences, of course, would not show
up in simple technical analyses, such as measuring, weighing,
or the like; but insofar as any science was a *theoretical* discipline,
Christians and non-Christians would reach some conclusions
that were different in important ways. Each would be equally
scientific, but they would be working from differing starting
points and frameworks of assumptions. So, said Kuyper, Christian and non-Christian scientific thinkers were not working on
different parts of the same building, but on different buildings.
Each "will of course claim for himself the high and noble name
of science, and withhold it from the other." Kuyper, who anticipated some of the insights of Thomas Kuhn (although working
from a much different philosophical base) was thus one of the
early challengers to the dream that had dominated so much of
modern Western thought—that the human race would eventually discover one body of objective scientific truth.[1]

To B. B. Warfield, Kuyper's view was sheer nonsense.
Warfield was a man of his age at least to the extent of believing
that science was an objective, unified, and cumulative enterprise of the entire race. "The human spirit," he said, "attains
this . . . by slow accretions, won through many partial and
erroneous constructions." In response to Kuyper, he maintained that "men of all sorts and of all grades work side by side
at the common task, and the common edifice grows under
their hands into ever fuller and truer outlines."[2] Warfield
differed from most of his contemporaries not in this classic

1. Abraham Kuyper, *Principles of Sacred Theology*, trans. J. Hendrik
De Vries (Grand Rapids: Baker Book House, 1980 [1898]), pp. 150-59.
2. Warfield, Introduction to Francis R. Beattie's *Apologetics: or the
Rational Vindication of Christianity* (Richmond, VA, 1903), in John E. Meeter,
ed., *Selected Shorter Writings of Benjamin B. Warfield*, II (Nutley, NJ: Presbyterian and Reformed Publishing Company, 1973), 101-02. These same
remarks appeared about the same time in a review of *De Zekerheid des
Geloofs* by Herman Bavinck in the *Princeton Theological Review*, January
1903, quoted in Warfield, *Shorter Writings*, II, 106-23.

view of science, but rather in his resistance to the recent trend to limit the meaning of "science" to the natural sciences and the new imitative social sciences. For Warfield and his colleagues at Princeton, theology was still the queen of the sciences and its truths could be discovered once and for all on the same foundational epistemological principles as the truths of Newtonian physics had been established.

Building on such assumptions, Warfield's confidence in demonstrating rationally the truths of Christianity knew no bounds. "It is not true," he insisted, "that he [the Christian] cannot soundly prove his position. It is not true that the Christian view of the world is subjective merely, and is incapable of validation in the forum of pure reason." Indeed, "All minds are of the same essential structure; and the less illuminated will not be able permanently to resist or gainsay the determination of the more illuminated." The reason of the regenerate, in fact, "shall ultimately conquer to itself the whole race." With such a prospect for total apologetic victory, Kuyper's insistence that science or rationality for the regenerate and for the unregenerate operated in differing frameworks seemed to Warfield to border on cowardice. As long as science was the common task of all people, said Warfield, "it is the better science that ever in the end wins the victory. . . . How shall it win its victory, however, if it declines the conflict?"[3]

In retrospect, this rhetoric seems of the ilk that might have sent Custer to the Little Bighorn. The Princetonians were fighting overwhelming odds but going down with their guns blazing. To them, however, it might not have been obvious how hopeless their position was. Only in 1902, for instance, had Warfield's good friend, theologian Francis L. Patton, retired as president of no less an academic center than Princeton University. Patton held the same views as Warfield on the simultaneous triumph of Calvinism and science. "Believing in Calvinism," Patton had proclaimed, "we believe that if Christendom shall have one unanimous faith, it will be the

3. Ibid., 103.

Calvinistic faith."[4] Patton was, however, part of a dying breed, one of the last clergymen presidents of a major American university. During his presidency, nonetheless, he had helped create the very scientifically specialized structures of the modern university that were making his own views such an anomaly. He and the other Princeton theologians remained confident that any structures that would help promote true science would in the long run promote true religion. So, far from seeing themselves as making a heroic last stand, they were confident that the forces of science, by which they were surrounded, were on their side.

THE HISTORICAL PROBLEM STATED

As they would have been the first to tell you, the strict Calvinist theologians at Princeton did not represent all of American evangelicalism. *Evangelicalism*, as I am using it here, refers to that broad movement, found especially in British and American Protestantism, that insisted that "the sole authority in religion is the Bible and the sole means of salvation is a life-transforming experience wrought by the Holy Spirit through faith in Jesus Christ."[5] Although the Princetonians were unhappy with many of the emphases of this broader evangelicalism, they nonetheless were allied with it and eventually became the intellectually most influential group in the conservative, or Bible-believing, evangelicalism that survived and now flourishes in the twentieth century. In fact, the Princetonians have been more influential in twentieth-century evangelicalism than they were among their nineteenth-century con-

4. Patton, *Speech . . . at the Annual Dinner of the Princeton Club in New York*, March 15, 1888 (New York, 1888), p. 5, quoted in Laurence R. Veysey, *The Emergence of the American University* (Chicago: University of Chicago Press, 1965), p. 52.

5. Grant Wacker, *Augustus H. Strong and the Dilemma of Historical Consciousness* (Macon, GA: Mercer University Press, 1985), p. 17. This is as economical and careful a definition as I have seen.

temporaries. The intellectual traits of this elite, then, although not exactly typical, represent unusually well-articulated tendencies that have resonated with the assumptions of an important segment of popular (white) evangelicalism, especially as it faced the secularizing threats of the twentieth century.

Why were the Princetonians and so many of their twentieth-century conservative, evangelical, intellectual dependents so committed in principle to a scientifically based culture even while the scientifically based culture of the twentieth century was undermining belief in the very truths of the Bible they held most dear? We cannot answer this question in its entirety, because it has many dimensions—theological, philosophical, psychological, sociological, institutional, and so forth. What this chapter does do, however, is to present a historical overview of the relationships between American evangelicalism and modern scientific culture, so that we can better understand the Princetonian and twentieth-century evangelical stance in terms of the tradition that nourished it.

EVANGELICALISM AND THE AMERICAN ENLIGHTENMENT

The crucial dimension of this American tradition becomes apparent if we ask what was centrally different about the cultural experiences that lay behind the outlooks of our two turn-of-the-century Calvinists, Abraham Kuyper and B. B. Warfield. Some similarities are immediately evident. Each of their nations had a predominantly Calvinist religious heritage. Each had been an early leader in tolerance and religious pluralism. Each had been much influenced by the Enlightenment and reshaped politically in the age of revolution.

The big difference, however, was in the Calvinists' relationship to the Enlightenment and revolution.[6] In Holland the

6. This idea was, I think, first suggested to me by Mark Noll.

Enlightenment had been associated largely with the secularism that had been on the rise since the seventeenth century. The Dutch revolution of the 1790s was widely regarded, at least by many Dutch Calvinists, as an outgrowth of the French Revolution and hence of "infidelity." During the first half of the nineteenth century, a pietist revival in the Netherlands paralleled the Second Great Awakening in the United States. The Dutch version of the revival eventually took the form of a "neo-Calvinist" resurgence. By the 1870s Abraham Kuyper had become leader of this formidable neo-Calvinist movement. For the next four decades he infused it with a vision of reforming all culture under Calvinist leadership. Kuyper eventually became an effective political leader because he recognized, in good Dutch fashion, that competing worldviews had their rights. But he often spoke of an "Antithesis" between a Calvinist worldview and contemporary worldviews controlled by the "humanism" and "materialism" growing out of the Enlightenment.[7] His Calvinist political party was called the "Anti-Revolutionary" party.

In the United States, it made a world of difference that Calvinists and their evangelical allies had been on the side of the American Revolution. This fact is crucial to understanding their view of the Enlightenment and their subsequent view of science. It is true that for a time after the French Revolution, some Calvinist leaders in the United States, most notably Yale President Timothy Dwight, raised an antirevolutionary flag in the name of Christianity versus Enlightenment "infidelity." Vestiges of this Dwightean viewpoint persisted throughout the next century (indeed, they survive today), so that many American evangelicals have spoken of "the Enlightenment" as synonymous with "rationalism" and "skepticism." This usage should not, however, lead us away from the true picture. Insofar as the Enlightenment represented an attitude toward rationality and scientific thinking, American evangelicals have

7. James D. Bratt, *Dutch Calvinism in Modern America: History of a Conservative Subculture* (Grand Rapids: Eerdmans, 1984), p. 21, cf. pp. 3-33.

been in many respects its champions, even while repudiating certain other tendencies in the eighteenth-century outlook.

Our understanding of this ambivalent, but essentially positive, relationship to Enlightenment thought is clarified, if we remember, as Henry May has taught us, that the Enlightenment in the United States had several manifestations. According to May, we can divide the European Enlightenment ideas that influenced the United States into four categories: First is the early Moderate Enlightenment associated with Newton and Locke—the ideals of order, balance, and religious compromise. Second is the Skeptical Enlightenment, represented best by Voltaire and Hume. Third is the Revolutionary Enlightenment—the search for a new heaven on earth—that grew out of the thought of Rousseau. And fourth is the Didactic Enlightenment, stemming from Scottish Common Sense thought, which opposed skepticism and revolution but rescued the essentials of the earlier eighteenth-century commitments to science, rationality, order, and the Christian tradition.

Of these four types of the Enlightenment, only the first and the fourth had major lasting influence in the United States. The American Revolution was managed primarily by proponents of the Moderate Enlightenment, such as Adams and Madison. More radical revolutionary ideas, such as those of Paine and Jefferson, were significant for a time, but were discredited in many influential circles when they became associated with the French Revolution and Paine's skepticism. Neither radical revolution nor Enlightenment skepticism took deep root in American culture. Instead, the Didactic Enlightenment of Scotland provided the basis for a synthesis.[8] According to the principles of Scottish philosophy, it appeared that the three great strands in American thought—modern empirical scientific ideals, the self-evident principles of the American Revolution, and evangelical Christianity—could be reconciled, or, rather, remain reconciled. Thus the Scottish Enlightenment

8. Henry F. May, *The Enlightenment in America* (New York: Oxford University Press, 1976), pp. xvi and passim.

had a remarkable afterlife in the United States, dominating American academic thought for the first six or seven decades of the nineteenth century.

In contrast to the situation in Europe, then, not only did an important component of the classic Enlightenment outlook survive, it was closely allied with biblically conservative evangelicalism. What lived was not any explicit commitment to the "Enlightenment" as such, but rather a dedication to the general philosophical basis that had undergirded the empirically based rationality so confidently proclaimed by most eighteenth-century thinkers. Thus, as many authors have observed, among the great heroes of the faith for evangelical intellectuals during the first half of the nineteenth century were Isaac Newton and Francis Bacon. Theodore Dwight Bozeman, in fact, documents the "beatification of Bacon," notably among those who were most theologically conservative.[9] This "beatification of Bacon" coincided with the Second Great Awakening. It helped provide for it a popular epistemology (as is evident in Charles Finney's insistence that producing a revival was just as scientific an enterprise as producing a crop of corn) and as a basis for Christian apologetics. So in the first heyday of evangelicalism in the United States, objective scientific thought was not tinged with the guilt of fostering secularism. Rather it was boldly lauded as the best friend of the Christian faith and of Christian culture generally.

This cordial relationship between Christianity and a scientifically based culture in the United States was, moreover, not a recent invention of the nineteenth century. Rather the synthesis of the Didactic Enlightenment was a matter of restoring a long-standing marriage briefly threatened by revolutionary passions and infidelity.

9. Theodore Dwight Bozeman, *Protestants in an Age of Science: The Baconian Ideal and Antebellum American Religious Thought* (Chapel Hill: University of North Carolina Press, 1977), pp. 72 and passim.

FAITH AND REASON

We should consider, however, the character of this well-known marriage of faith and science if we are to understand what went on later. Concerning its beginnings, we know, of course, that the Puritans cordially supported the new science of the seventeenth century. Although, on the one hand, the scientific outlook might have seemed to create a tension with the Puritans' providential readings of nature, on the other hand, the Puritans were so preoccupied with their understanding of God as an orderly lawgiver that they welcomed and fostered investigation of that orderliness.

By the eighteenth century, however, the tension between providential and natural law explanations was becoming a major struggle for thoughtful Protestants of all sorts.[10] Probably it is safe to say that even many of those who were theologically orthodox adopted a worldview that, in effect, had Deist tendencies. They viewed the universe as a machine run by natural laws, and in practice distanced the Creator from their understandings of the everyday operations of creation.[11] They also made a sharper distinction between the natural and the supernatural. Those who remained more or less orthodox tended simultaneously to view natural events in two ways, which they considered simply complementary perspectives.[12] Because God was the author of all that was, what he revealed through natural law would always harmonize with special rev-

10. James Turner, *Without God, Without Creed: The Origin of Unbelief in America* (Baltimore: Johns Hopkins University Press, 1985), p. 39, provides a nice example of James Boswell's personal wrestling with this issue in 1764.

11. Jonathan Edwards is an example of someone who took the opposite approach, as in his "Dissertation Concerning the End for which God Created the World."

12. Turner, *Without God,* pp. 39-40, illustrates this dual outlook in the remarks of Charles Chauncy on the New England earthquake of 1755 as both a law-governed natural event and warning from God. Turner, although sometimes given to hyperbole, furnishes a helpful version of the present thesis.

elation. The two revelations, indeed, paralleled each other, as Bishop Butler argued. Moreover, as William Paley eventually put it in what became its classic statement, empirical science supported Scripture by providing irrefutable evidence of design.

By the end of the eighteenth century, American Protestants of almost all sorts had adopted this two-tiered worldview, founded on an empiricist epistemology, with the laws of nature below, supporting supernatural belief above. They thus had worked out a modern version of the Thomist synthesis of reason and faith. Or, in H. Richard Niebuhr's categories, they had worked out a "Christ Above Culture" intellectual framework in which the realism of science and faith could not conflict.[13]

We can get a glimpse of how this harmonious two-tiered worldview worked if we look for a moment at late eighteenth-century Christian views of what we today would call the social sciences. At the time of the American Revolution in the eighteenth century, most Americans viewed political thought as an empirically based scientific discipline, in the tradition of John Locke. What is striking about the eighteenth-century evangelical Christian views of the matter (especially if we contrast them with the immense twentieth-century literature of Christian views of politics) is that there is no distinctly Christian view of political science in the revolutionary era. Rather (excepting perhaps the sectarians) eighteenth-century American Christians offered no distinct perspectives on revolutionary theory.[14] Patriotic Christian Americans could accept without criticism the political theories of Jefferson or Paine. When it got to the realm of "spiritual" questions, they would, of course, part ways. But on mundane matters they assumed that political science was identical for the Christian and the non-Christian. Moreover, many of the truths found by natural law could be

13. H. Richard Niebuhr, *Christ and Culture* (New York: Harper & Row, 1951).
14. Mark A. Noll, *Christians in the American Revolution* (Grand Rapids: Christian University Press, 1977).

confirmed by supernatural revelation. The self-evident injustice of taxation without representation, for instance, confirmed the divine revelation, "Thou shalt not steal." Locke's contract theory of government was, in practice, sufficiently like the Puritan covenant that no one in the revolutionary era seems to have thought it significant to criticize its essentially secular theoretical base.

This modern Protestant counterpart to the Thomist synthesis of science and faith was preserved and expanded in the days of American evangelical intellectual hegemony during the first half of the nineteenth century. Francis Wayland, the Baptist author of the most popular college textbooks of the era, provides a typical example. In his *Elements of Moral Science* (1835) he argues that ethics is as much a science as physics, each discovering laws of sequences of cause and effect. Inductive science, however, can go only so far in discovering moral principles. So God's additional revelation in the Bible is necessary to supplement what reason tells us (adding, for instance, information about the Incarnation or the Atonement) and to point us to some moral principles built into nature (such as the value of one day's rest in seven) that we might not have noticed otherwise. Scripture and rational moral science operating independently will reveal completely harmonious principles. The harmony of these two independent sources of truth, says Wayland, constitutes firm evidence for the Christian religion. "So complete is this coincidence," he exclaims, "as to afford irrefragable proof that the Bible contains the moral laws of the universe; and hence, that the Author of the universe—that is of natural religion—is also the Author of the Scriptures."[15]

---

15. Francis Wayland, *Elements of Moral Science*, ed. Joseph Angus (London, ca. 1860 [1835]), pp. 219-20.

I have used this example and those in the next four paragraphs in another context (and in a place where only philosophers are likely to see them) in "The Collapse of American Evangelical Academia," in Alvin Plantinga and Nicholas Wolterstorff, eds., *Faith and Rationality* (South Bend: University of Notre Dame Press, 1984). A few of the other themes in this essay are also found in that one.

Consistent with this two-level approach to truth, Wayland could take an entirely different approach in his subsequent text *The Elements of Political Economy* (1837). Although he acknowledges that most topics in political economy could be discussed also in moral philosophy, he writes that "he [Wayland] has not thought it proper to intermingle them, but has argued economical questions on merely economical grounds." Political economy, in other words, is a pure science and has "nothing to do" with ethical questions.[16]

In retrospect, Wayland's approach has been seen as part of a subtle process of secularization in American life. Martin Marty, for instance, points out that secularization typically took place through a peaceful separation of "religious areas" in American life from the secular and the scientific. When this division of labor took place, the two realms were seen in perfect harmony, and true science was always the base of proof for true religion.[17] Once the disciplines were declared autonomous and separated from explicit Christian reference until after they had drawn their conclusions, however, it was easy for a later generation to omit altogether the latter step of reference to Christianity.

In the natural sciences, the pattern was both similar and more dramatic. The Baconian methodology in the natural sciences provided the model that the emerging social sciences attempted to imitate. In the natural sciences, however, it was more difficult to see what relationship Christianity would have with most of the technical aspects of the enterprise, even if one wished to relate the two. Generally, evangelical American scientists assumed the total objectivity of their enterprise, but then related it to their Christianity by noting the harmonies of scientific truth and truth in the higher realms of religion and morality. Perhaps the most common way of relating Christianity to science was the "doxological." One should emerge from

16. Wayland, *The Elements of Political Economy* (Boston, 1860 [1837]), p. iv.

17. Martin E. Marty, *The Modern Schism: Three Paths to the Secular* (New York: Harper & Row, 1969), p. 98.

one's scientific inquiries into nature praising God for the marvels of his creation.[18]

Closely related, but more important for our purposes, was the apologetic use of natural science. In addition to the foundational argument from design, these arguments pointed out the harmonies between what was known in the natural world and what was known in the moral and spiritual world. *"The theology of natural science,"* declared Lewis W. Green in 1854, in a typical statement of the day, "is in perfect harmony with *the theology of the Bible.*" Each of these, plus our moral intuitions, told us of a wise, benevolent, and orderly governor of the universe. The harmonious fit of the Bible with what was discovered by objective science in these other areas was the crucial question for the evangelical apologists. Their principal opponents were Deists who shared their beliefs that the natural and moral order pointed inescapably to a wise deity. The Bible, the evangelical apologists were convinced, could be shown to fit exactly with objective truths discovered in these other areas. As Mark Hopkins, the best-known evangelical teacher of the era, put it in summarizing his apologetics: "There is a harmony of adaptation, and also of analogy. The key is adapted to the lock; the fin of the fish is analogous to the wing of the bird. Christianity, as I hope to show, is adapted to man." Given such parallels and harmonies in the two sources of revelation, said Lewis Green in 1854, Christians had nothing to fear if astronomy discovered new worlds, geology new ages, or anthropology extinct races and species. Rather would "the Christian welcome joyfully, and appropriate each successive revelation."[19]

18. Bozeman, *Protestants in an Age of Science;* George H. Daniels, *American Science in the Age of Jackson* (New York: Columbia University Press, 1968); Herbert Hovenkamp, *Science and Religion in America, 1800-1860* (Philadelphia: University of Pennsylvania Press, 1978); E. Brooks Holifield, *The Gentlemen Theologians: American Theology in Southern Culture, 1795-1860* (Durham: Duke University Press, 1978).

19. Lewis W. Green, *Lectures on the Evidences of Christianity* (New York, 1854), pp. 463-64; Mark Hopkins, *Evidence of Christianity* (Boston, 1876 [1846]), p. 75.

THE DARWINIAN CHALLENGES

The reception of Darwinism, which eventually became pivotal in shaping and symbolizing evangelical attitudes toward scientific culture, has to be understood in this context. By 1859, evangelicals, both scientists and theologians, thought they had discovered an impregnable synthesis between faith and reason. Scientific reasoning, the kind they most respected, firmly supported Christian faith. In principle they were deeply wedded to a scientific culture, so long as it left room (indeed, a privileged place of honor) to add on their version of Christianity.

Given this commitment, it is not surprising that the evangelical reaction to Darwinism was, as numerous recent studies have shown,[20] far more ambivalent than the stereotyped story would suggest. The stereotyped story, so convenient to those of us who lecture about modern culture, has been framed by the metaphors of warfare. According to this story, Darwinism marked the triumphant assault of modern scientific culture against the last remaining citadels of the premodern religious culture. In England, the story goes, the fulminations of Bishop Wilberforce typified the consternation of the befuddled defenders of traditional religion. Thomas Huxley, however, destroyed Wilberforce's position in their famed debate of 1860. After that it was a mopping-up operation, although fundamentalists remained here and there, especially here in America, for many years after. This version of the story has been tagged "1859 and All That."[21] The implication of the story is that

20. E.g., James R. Moore, *The Post-Darwinian Controversies: A Study of the Protestant Struggle to Come to Terms with Darwin in Great Britain and America, 1870-1900* (Cambridge: Cambridge University Press, 1979); Neil C. Gillespie, *Charles Darwin and the Problem of Creation* (Chicago: University of Chicago Press, 1979); Peter J. Bowler, *Evolution: The History of an Idea* (Berkeley: University of California Press, 1984); John Durant, ed., *Darwinism and Divinity: Essays on Evolution and Religious Belief* (Oxford: Basil Blackwell, 1985); Ronald L. Numbers, "Science and Religion," *OSIRIS* 1, 2d series (1985), 59-80.

21. James R. Moore, "1859 and All That: Remaking the Story of Evolution and Religion," in Roger G. Chapman and Cleveland T. Duval,

Darwinism brought the decisive culmination of a long-standing struggle between modernity and prescientific religious faith.

In fact, because evangelicalism and the scientific culture had been so deeply intertwined throughout the first half of the nineteenth century, the reactions to Darwinism were far more complex. One evidence of this is that opinions about Darwinism did not immediately split exactly along conservative and liberal theological lines. Although it is possible that lay opinion among strict Bible-believers was largely negative regarding biological evolution,[22] the conservative intellectual leadership was divided. While various conservative leaders pointed out a number of problems with reconciling Christianity and Darwinism, others (just as conservative) proposed ways of surmounting these problems.

The first of the problems for conservative Bible-believers was that of reconciling biological evolution with a literal interpretation of early Genesis. This question, however, did not cause the polarization that (in light of current discussion by "creation scientists")[23] we might expect. The way had been prepared during the first half of the century by extensive intraevangelical debates over how to reconcile Genesis with the seemingly inescapable evidence for geological evolution[24] and the more speculative, but popular, nebular hypothesis for explaining the natural origins of the universe.[25] Although there were holdouts,[26] the predominant opinion among American

---

eds., *Charles Darwin, 1809-1882: A Centennial Commemorative* (Wellington, New Zealand: Nova Pacifica, 1982), pp. 167-94.

22. Numbers, "Science and Religion," p. 73.

23. See Chapter 6.

24. Bowler, *Evolution*, p. 206.

25. Ronald L. Numbers, *Creation by Natural Law: Laplace's Nebular Hypothesis in American Thought* (Seattle: University of Washington Press, 1977).

26. These holdouts were not necessarily obscurantists. See, for instance, the view of Moses Stuart, a champion of modern scientific methods of biblical scholarship as discussed in George M. Marsden, "Everyone One's Own Interpreter? The Bible, Science, and Authority in Mid-Nineteenth Century America," in Nathan O. Hatch and Mark A.

conservative evangelical leaders was that Genesis was susceptible to some reinterpretation in the light of modern scientific
discovery. By the time *Origin of Species* appeared, the commonplace view among biblicists was that the six "days" of creation
in the first chapter of Genesis represented vast eons. Moreover,
the order of the creation of the species in Genesis fit roughly
the Darwinian order. As to whether God might create through
evolutionary means, there was no new problem. If God could
guide the natural evolution of mountains, he could create
other entities that way.

A second objection was the "dignity of man" argument,
proposed by Bishop Wilberforce and many others who were
offended by thinking of humans and apes as blood relations.
Such initial objections were not confined to biblicists. Biblicist
evolutionists, moreover, could easily sidestep the substantive
aspect of this objection by proposing that God may have inter-
vened late in the evolutionary process, either to create humans
as a distinct species or at least to create the human soul.

A third type of objection to Darwinism was based on
scientific considerations. Initially, however, these did not follow
conservative-versus-liberal theological lines either. The most
formidable American scientific opponent of Darwin was Harvard's Louis Agassiz, a Unitarian. The most formidable supporter was Agassiz's colleague, Asa Gray, an evangelical. Most
American evangelicals had a firm commitment to nonspecula-
tive Baconian inductionism, and some objected to Darwin's
speculations on those grounds. By the 1870s, however, many
evangelical scientists were following Gray in seeing that Darwin's hypothesis explained too many disparate phenomena to
be lightly dismissed as a working model.[27]

A fourth objection was more philosophical. It was best
articulated by Charles Hodge of Princeton Theological Seminary. Hodge's objection was summarized in the conclusion to

---

Noll, eds., *The Bible in America: Essays in Cultural History* (New York: Oxford
University Press, 1982), pp. 92-93.

27. Cf. note 20 above.

his 1874 study *What is Darwinism?* "What is Darwinism?" Hodge asked. "It is atheism." Hodge's summary so well suits the warfare model for understanding the relation of conservative religion and post-Darwinian science that it has been a favorite quotation supposedly encapsulating the conservative side of the whole affair. In fact, however, Hodge was making some careful distinctions. The idea of evolution, he observed, was not unique to Darwin, nor was that the important point at issue. Neither was the concept of natural selection. What was central and crucial, said Hodge, was that "Darwin rejects all teleology, or the doctrine of final causes." To Hodge, Darwin's intransigence on this point amounted to a practical atheism, because it left us with a chance universe.[28]

The great debate within the American (and British) evangelical community was whether Darwin's total rejection of design was *entailed* by his theories about biological development or whether they were views that were nonessential to true "Darwinism." Asa Gray and Darwin corresponded at length on this point and never did agree.[29] Among conservative Protestant intellectuals, however, the prevailing opinion seems to have favored Gray's view, thus allowing for reconciliation of some version of Darwin's biological theories with the Bible, and hence design.[30] Liberal evangelicals managed this by adopting ever-looser interpretations of Scripture. Many conservatives, however, reconciled themselves to at least limited versions of biological evolution without giving up their trust in biblical reliability. Except in the South in the late nineteenth century opposition to evolution was seldom made a test of evangelical faith.[31]

28. Charles Hodge, *What is Darwinism?* (New York: Scribners, Armstrong, and Company, 1874), excerpts in Mark A. Noll, editor and compiler, *The Princeton Theology, 1812-1921* (Grand Rapids: Baker Book House, 1983), pp. 145-52.

29. Moore, *Post-Darwinian Controversies*, pp. 269-80.

30. Cf. note 20 above.

31. See Chapter 6 and also David N. Livingstone, *Darwin's Forgotten Defenders: The Encounter between Evangelical Theology and Evolutionary Thought* (Grand Rapids: Eerdmans, 1987), pp. 115-21.

ORIGINS OF THE CONFLICT

How, then, did the conservative evangelical reaction to Darwinism come to be regarded as though it always had been an all-out warfare, when for a half-century the attitudes among some of the movement's most prominent leaders were, at least, mixed and ambivalent? The answer to this question will give us an important clue to identifying where the real tension point was developing between evangelicals and the new scientific culture.

A number of recent historians of the reception of Darwinism seem largely agreed that, in the early decades after *Origin of Species*, the "warfare" framework for understanding the relationship of Christianity to Darwinism was developed and promoted primarily by ardent opponents of Christianity.[32] A few defenders of Christianity did immediately anathematize Darwinism, and some, as in the American South, continued to do so. The anti-Christian polemicists, however, made the most of such opposition, suggesting that traditional Christians had always attacked modern science. In short, they claimed, this was another instance of a long-standing war between faith and science. Soon after Darwin published, his defenders vigorously promoted this warfare metaphor. In 1869, for instance, Andrew Dixon White, the young president of Cornell, lectured a New York City audience on "The Battle-Fields of Science." White's version of the story eventually developed into his two-volume *History of the Warfare of Science with Theology in Christendom* (1896). In the meantime, John William Draper's popular *History of the Conflict between Religion and Science* (1874) had already introduced a large reading public to the warfare model. Both White and Draper projected the warfare into the past. Through dubious reconstructions of the evidence (usu-

32. Ibid., pp. 19-102; John Durant, "Darwinism and Divinity: A Century of Debate," in Durant, ed., *Darwinism and Divinity*, pp. 9-39; and Ronald L. Numbers, "Science and Religion," each summarize some of the other sources in this growing consensus.

ally ignoring, for instance, that most of the debates about science had been debates among Christians)[33] they suggested that the intellectual life of the past several centuries had been dominated by the conflict between advocates of religiously based obscurantism and enlightened champions of value-free scientific truth.

One does not have to look far to see what was behind such heavy-handed reconstructions of the past. White and Draper were prophets of a new age in which the scientific quest for truth would finally be freed from religious constraint. As prophets tend to, they saw the issue as a contest between the forces of light and the forces of darkness. The prototype of this company of prophets was "Darwin's Bulldog," T. H. Huxley. Huxley was preoccupied with the metaphors of warfare for describing his efforts. "Warfare has been my business and duty," he declared frankly. Huxley spoke for that band of intellectual "agnostics" (to use his new term) who were convinced that people should not be guided by beliefs they could not know with scientific certainty. They were champions of essentially Auguste Comte's view that positive science must replace inferior ways that civilizations had previously used to find truth. To do this, the essential first step was the reform of science itself, to remove it from any connection with religion. Science must be defined as the investigation of natural causes and nothing else. Science that continued to have the traditional references to religion must be called nonscience. As Neil Gillespie summarizes it, the older "episteme" open to religious truth had to be discredited, because "the very existence of a rival science or of an alternate mode of knowledge was intolerable to the positivist." For a Huxley or a Draper, says Gillespie, "It was not enough to drive out the old ideas. Their

33. David C. Lindberg and Ronald L. Numbers, "Beyond War and Peace: A Reappraisal of the Encounter between Christianity and Science," *Church History* 55 (September 1986), 338-54. Cf., by the same authors, *God and Nature: Historical Essays on the Encounter between Christianity and Science* (Berkeley: University of California Press, 1986).

advocates had to be driven out of the scientific community as well.[34]

Two well-known points about this campaign should be briefly noted. First, this effort to secularize both science and society was under way before Darwin published. Second, the secularizers accepted Darwin's views so enthusiastically and promoted them so vigorously because they were ideally suited to their campaign. Darwin's massive array of evidence was aimed directly at the concept of design, the link between Christianity and science that had been hardest to dissolve. Once science was freed, civilization could be. As T. H. Huxley said characteristically in a review of Darwin's theory in 1860, "Every philosophical thinker hails it as a veritable Whitworth gun in the armoury of liberalism."[35]

WHY MANY BIBLICISTS DID NOT KNOW THEY WERE AT WAR WITH SCIENCE

Darwinism appeared, of course, at a time when there was a widespread impulse toward secularization in Western culture. It is important to note that so far as secularization was something that was advocated, in addition to something that just happened, it could have two very different rationales. On the one hand, the push to secularize might come from nonreligious people, such as the agnostics, who were convinced that their positivism (using the term loosely) provided a better moral basis for civilization than did Christianity.[36] On the other hand, secularization might be promoted simply

34. Gillespie, *Charles Darwin*, pp. 152-53.
35. Thomas Henry Huxley, "Orthodoxy Scotched, If Not Slain," abridged from Huxley, *Lay Sermons, Addresses, and Reviews* (New York, 1871), in Harold Y. Vanderpool, ed., *Darwin and Darwinism: Revolutionary Insights concerning Man, Nature, Religion, and Society* (Lexington, MA: D. C. Heath, 1973), p. 91.
36. Turner, *Without God*, discusses the conviction of the agnostics that their position was essential to a higher morality (e.g., p. 203).

as a methodology. That is, various activities might be removed from religious reference not because people sought
to promote a non-Christian worldview, but simply because
people were convinced that the activities could be better
carried out without the distractions of religious considerations, however valuable those considerations might be in
other contexts. As we have seen, evangelicals in the United
States had already been advocating methodological secularization, à la Francis Wayland. Moreover, to return to Martin
Marty's point, secularization in this country initially involved
relatively little antireligious sentiment.[37] So in the latter decades of the nineteenth century many biblicist Christians
might advocate the methodological secularization of science
for many of the same reasons that they might favor the trend
toward more efficient business practices.[38] So they might
have been ready allies of the militant agnostics in the campaign to get religion out of science, that is, to define science
purely naturalistically.[39]

Such methodological secularization was connected with
the professionalization of American life. Professionalization involved the isolation of various disciplines. One of the natural
implications of this isolation of the disciplines was that theology
would have to be isolated from each of them. All this fit with
sentiments to make each discipline more scientific and to define science naturalistically. The trend was reinforced by the
need simply to improve scientific study itself. In pre–Civil War
America, much natural science, for instance, had been conducted by amateurs, often theologians. A more strictly naturalistic definition of science was thus likely to appeal to those

37. Marty, *Modern Schism*, passim. Marty points out, for instance,
the contrast with the anticlericalism in French secularization.

38. Samuel Haber, *Efficiency and Uplift: Scientific Management in the
Progressive Era, 1890-1920* (Chicago: University of Chicago Press, 1964),
suggests a widespread American enthusiasm (in which conservative evangelicals apparently participated) for "scientific" procedures of all sorts
during this era.

39. Cf. Gillespie, *Charles Darwin*, p. 13.

Christians or non-Christians who thought that quality would be improved by developing professional specialties.

The rise of the social sciences followed similar lines. As American universities emerged after the Civil War, the new social sciences were organized on a scientific model. William Graham Sumner provides a familiar example of the new secular outlook. His famous remark—that he put his religious beliefs in a drawer and twenty years later he opened the drawer and the beliefs were gone—illustrates the ease with which a secularized methodology might be turned into a secular worldview.

Sumner, however, was not typical of American academics in the 1870s. Rather, both in the natural sciences and in the social sciences, it took a whole generation for the transition to take place. Until at least around the turn of the century, the moral-religious tradition that had been inherited from the amateur practitioners of moral science and political economy retained some momentum. So, for instance, we find the early literature of the American Economic Association, founded in 1886, describing it as a Christian endeavor. Richard T. Ely, the first secretary, declared at the organizational meeting that because "our work lies in the direction of practical Christianity, we appeal to the church, the chief of the social forces in this country, to help us, to support us, and to make our work a complete success, which it can by no possibility be without her assistance." Apparently not all the organizers agreed with this sentiment. Just as important, the papers presented to the early organization were strictly technical.[40] Because the discipline was thus defined as a science, it would be relatively simple in the next generation to let views such as Ely's simply die out.

Prior to 1900 the apparently benign nature of American secularization kept most conservative evangelicals from seeing

40. "Statement of Dr. Richard T. Ely," *Report of the Organization of the American Economic Association,* Richard T. Ely, Secretary, vol. I, no. 1 (Baltimore, 1886), p. 18. Cf. the footnote on p. 14 that, although some endorsed his views without reservation, others objected strongly, so that Ely's views did not officially represent the association. Cf. passim.

what was taking place. One thing that confused the issue was that evangelical Protestantism was now breaking into liberal and conservative camps. So conservatives, who might approve of relating Christianity to social analyses when it was done by conservatives, might disapprove of it when done by theological liberals. Moreover, they were still free in their own circles to promote their own views about Christian economic and social principles, an exercise that may have contributed to the illusion that they were still speaking to the whole nation.[41] Indeed, the alliance between Christian rhetoric and politics was still taken for granted at the center of American public life through the Progressive Era. In the triumph of Prohibition in 1919 the conservative and liberal wings of Protestantism allied for one last nationwide victory, but they, of course, had no way of knowing it was their last. Such victories, or the hopes for them, could keep alive the belief that conservative Christians still had an important voice in controlling the science-infatuated American culture.

AND THEN IT WAS TOO LATE

Such continuing influences of evangelical Christianity on public life obscured the degree to which conservative Christians were completely losing their place in some of the crucial centers of the scientific culture. Sometime after 1900, probably after 1910, the isolation of the sciences from religious considerations, especially from the academically discredited conservative biblicist views, had become no longer an option but a strict requirement. The trend had advanced so far that there was no longer any way for conservative Bible-believers to have a voice for their religious views within a scientific discipline.

41. Gary Scott Smith, *The Seeds of Secularization: Calvinism, Culture, and Pluralism in America, 1870-1915* (Grand Rapids: Christian University Press, 1985), documents the close attention that Calvinist leaders gave to national issues and their ongoing hopes to influence them decisively.

In American academe there was one science indeed, and biblicist Christianity had no part in it. Moreover, by now it had become the intellectual fashion to abandon the Christian faith. So the naturalistic definition of science was rapidly being transformed from a methodology into a dominant academic worldview.

This brings us back to the debate between Warfield and Kuyper. The strategy of the American evangelicals, which was built on the assumption that there was one set of scientific truths for the whole race and hence that the best views ought eventually to drive out those that were inferior, set up the American evangelicals for their spectacular intellectual defeat. The attitudes of the Princetonians again illustrate the point. All through the later decades of the nineteenth century they had been noting and deploring the secularization of various areas of American life. A. A. Hodge, for instance, had warned in 1877 against the consequences of removing biblical teachings from public school textbooks, as in eliminating references to Providence and faith in the study of history, or in studying society without regard for biblical principles concerning the moral order. But as Gary Scott Smith has pointed out in his study of American Calvinists' response to secularization, such intellectual Protestants did not recognize that equity might demand that major competing worldviews be given more or less equal places in public life. Rather, their concept of a free republic was one in which one view would triumph in free competition. In economic terms, they would have expected the triumph of a monopoly. Because 90 percent of Americans were Christians, argued A. A. Hodge (in a rare display of generosity to Catholics and liberal Protestants), the government and the schools should be based on explicitly Christian principles. As Smith argues, this attitude that there should be a monolithic public philosophy dominating the public schools opened the door for the triumph of a secular version of such a policy.[42]

42. Smith, *Seeds of Secularization,* pp. 40-41, 77, and 93.

The emergence of John Dewey as America's philosopher in the first half of the twentieth century pointedly illustrates the nature of the transition. It is immensely illuminating to realize, as Bruce Kuklick has been emphasizing, that Dewey was a New England Calvinist at heart. His "common faith," promoted through the established school system, can thus be viewed as a secular version of the ideals of the New England standing order.

It is also illuminating to see how Dewey's views changed with the academic winds of his era. Until the 1890s, Dewey, like many American academics, related his philosophizing to Christian faith. By the early twentieth century, however, we find Dewey as a champion of a virtual Comtean positivism, praising the triumph of "science" over religious prejudice. Thus Dewey became the archetypal spokesman of his time, marking the triumph of a positivist definition of science that excluded religious reference.[43]

The way in which the seemingly benign nature of American secularization apparently shielded conservative American evangelicals from the imminent triumph of such views until it was too late is most dramatically illustrated in natural science. As we have seen, in the first generation after Darwin, a substantial number of both theologians and scientists were debating exactly how Darwinism might be reconciled with traditional biblical faith. Neil Gillespie argues that during this generation there were two competing "epistemes" within the scientific community, one that viewed such traditional questions of reconciliation of science to the Bible as relevant, and another that saw them as wildly irrelevant and illegitimate.[44] By about 1910, however, the generation of scientists who thought it legitimate to talk about such issues had, in good Kuhnian fashion, simply died out. One of the last to go was

43. E.g., Dewey, "Science in the Reconstruction of Philosophy" (1920), in Loren Baritz, ed., *Sources of the American Mind*, II (New York: Joseph Wiley & Sons, Inc., 1966), 19.
44. Gillespie, *Charles Darwin*.

Oberlin College's George Frederick Wright, a protégé of Asa Gray, a respected (though amateur) geologist, a conservative reconciler of evolution and early Genesis, and eventually a contributor to *The Fundamentals*. Wright died in 1921 at the age of eighty-three. He was the last of a species.

At the Scopes trial in 1925, Clarence Darrow asked William Jennings Bryan whether he could name any reputable scientist who shared his views. Bryan feebly replied that he thought there was someone named Wright at Oberlin and then named George McCready Price. Darrow was waiting for this part of the answer. Price was a thoroughly amateur proponent of Seventh-Day Adventist Ellen White's view that the Genesis flood explained the earth's geological formations. Darrow could retort with some confidence that "every scientist in this country knows [he] is a mountebank and a pretender and not a geologist at all."[45]

THE FUNDAMENTALIST WAR ON EVOLUTION

The disappearance by the 1920s of biblicist views in virtually all the sciences makes it less surprising that at this point "evolution" emerged among conservative evangelicals (now called fundamentalists) as the almost universal unifying symbol of everything that was wrong. For the fundamentalists, as for the positivists earlier, "evolution" took on truly mythical proportions as the all-explanatory symbol of scientific naturalism.[46] The fundamentalist leaders who opposed evolution recognized that evolutionism had to do with more than just a theory about biology. Evolutionism reflected, and for many champions of secularism long had symbolized, an entire naturalistic worldview. In this worldview, all talk of absolutes had

45. Ronald L. Numbers, "Creationism in 20th-Century America," *Science* 218/5 (November 1982), 540.
46. David N. Livingstone, "Evolution as Myth and Metaphor," *Christian Scholar's Review* 12 (1983), 11-25, expands the theme of the mythological function of evolution in modern culture.

been dissolved by the widespread conviction that the best way, the only scientific way, to understand things was through historical or developmental explanations. Biblical criticism, which had done so much to discredit traditional evangelical faith, was based on such premises. Conservative evangelical scholars, who a generation earlier had hoped to participate in the science of historical criticism while retaining traditional evangelical faith, were now finding that they had to choose.[47] The thoroughly naturalistic premises of the historicism that had come to dominate the field were consistent only with naturalistic conclusions.

"Evolution," then, became for fundamentalists the chief symbol of their warfare with modern scientific culture. Increasingly, for instance, the fundamentalist subculture would tolerate no concessions to biological evolution. As they almost always made clear, however, they were still not opposed to science as such. They favored what they regarded as true objective science, and they opposed only the biased, false, naturalistic-historicist science that dominated the age.[48]

The period from about 1920 to 1950 became a sort of academic dark age for conservative evangelical scholarship. Biblical considerations had been ruled out of bounds in the sciences, so in the northern United States explicitly biblicist evangelical scholars virtually disappeared from those fields. Secularists were enjoying the heyday of positivism, and Jewish scholars, emerging as a major force in American intellectual life, understandably had strong interest in eliminating vestiges of "Christian civilization," which they associated with the lethal anti-Semitism of the era. Although traditionalist biblicist Christians held college or university posts here and there, explicitly evangelical scholarship was largely in exile.

47. Wacker, *Augustus H. Strong and the Dilemma of Historical Consciousness,* provides a dramatic example of this struggle in a major biblicist evangelical leader of the era.

48. George M. Marsden, *Fundamentalism and American Culture: The Shaping of Twentieth-Century Evangelicalism, 1870-1925* (New York: Oxford University Press, 1980), esp. pp. 212-21.

The institutional manifestation of this academic exile was the accelerating growth of the Bible Institute movement. In place of the network of colleges dominated by evangelicals in the nineteenth century, fundamentalists during the first half of the twentieth century were building a network of Bible Institutes, practical training centers in which the curricula centered on the Bible alone. In these schools they learned from other disciplines only insofar as these might aid in evangelism and missions. Fundamentalists still talked about being scientific; but in fact they had become almost thoroughly isolated and alienated from the dominant American scientific culture. Warfare was now indeed the appropriate metaphor for understanding their relationship to the scientific culture.

THE SEQUEL: WARFIELD AND KUYPER TODAY

The story does not end there. If the era from 1920 to 1950 was a dark age for conservative evangelical scholarship, the period since 1950 has been a time of minor renaissance. After World War II, some of the heirs to fundamentalism consciously attempted to promote an intellectual comeback.

Most roots of the resurgence can be traced to the tradition of the Princeton theologians, the one group in the fundamentalist coalition who had insisted on rigorous scholarship. J. Gresham Machen, a New Testament scholar respected even by many of his opponents, had led the Princeton movement during the years of fundamentalist-modernist controversies. Eventually, in 1929, Machen had been forced out of Princeton Seminary and had founded his own theological school, Westminster Theological Seminary in Philadelphia. In the 1930s most of the few serious scholars who remained in fundamentalism had some connection with Machen. These inspired a new generation of fundamentalist intellectuals who began to emerge by the early 1940s. A notable number of these aspiring academics did graduate work at Harvard. Many of these scholars were associated with the National Association of Evangelicals (NAE), an agency founded in 1942, primarily to foster intrafundamentalist unity, to promote evangelism, and to try to regain a hearing in American life.

As we have seen in Chapter 2, these scholarly fundamentalists, or "new evangelicals," as they came to be called, emphasized the need to meet the intellectual challenges of the age if the movement was to have a lasting impact.[49]

These emphases accompanied important sociological changes in the movement. The evangelicals who were breaking away from strict fundamentalism were somewhat more affluent and, like many Americans after World War II, more interested in college education. Many of their young people were now attending colleges, and by the 1960s substantial numbers were emerging from graduate schools. Some gained university positions and others staffed a growing number of evangelical colleges. By the 1970s "evangelicalism" referred to a wide variety of denominational orientations. The Christian College Coalition, for instance, reflected this diversity. By the 1980s it was serving some seventy member colleges. Evangelical scholars from these schools and from universities not only participated in the professional societies of their disciplines but also founded their own parallel societies and journals. Of these, the Society of Christian Philosophers, within the American Philosophical Association, has been most impressive, including in its membership some of the leading figures in the field. The collective literary production of evangelical scholars has developed into a minor industry.[50]

If we look at this evangelical renaissance as an intellectual movement, one theme overshadows all others. In virtually every field the principal intraevangelical debate has been the

49. George M. Marsden, *Reforming Fundamentalism: Fuller Seminary and the New Evangelicalism* (Grand Rapids: Eerdmans, 1987), explores this phase of the movement.

50. Mark Lau Branson, *The Reader's Guide to the Best Evangelical Books* (San Francisco: Harper & Row, 1982), provides a survey of some of this scholarship.

same: Do evangelical Christian scholars pursue their science or discipline differently from the way secularists do? By now the literature on this subject is vast.[51] In almost every field today, evangelical scholars are divided basically into two camps, with some hybrids in between. These camps are the Warfieldians and the Kuyperians, although they do not necessarily identify themselves as such or follow their mentors precisely. The Warfieldians—those who believe in one science or rationality on which all humanity ought to agree—point to the breakdown of any promised consensus in secular twentieth-century thought and claim that evangelical Christians can still argue their way to victory, at least in individual cases. To do so, they must stay on common ground with the non-Christians as long as possible, pursuing the technical aspects of their disciplines with just the same methodologies as their secular contemporaries do, but adding to them Christian moral and theological principles that truly objective people will see are rationally necessary to complete the picture. The Kuyperians, in contrast, emphasize that any discipline is built on starting assumptions and that Christians' basic assumptions should have substantial effects on many of their theoretical conclusions in a discipline. Thus two conflicting worldviews may be scientific or rational if each is consistent with its starting premises. People who start with premises that exclude God as an explanatory force and people who start with belief in God as among their basic beliefs may be equally rational and may be able to work together on technical scientific enterprises; but on some key theoretical issues their best arguments will simply come to opposed conclusions.[52] There will be two or more sciences. Rationality alone will not be able to settle arguments among them.

At the moment the issues in the intraevangelical debate

---

51. *Christian Scholar's Review*, founded in 1971 and supported by some thirty Christian colleges and universities, has provided one of the major forums of these discussions.

52. See Plantinga and Wolterstorff, eds., *Faith and Rationality*, for philosophical discussion of these issues.

are far from resolved. The Warfieldians still look back, in effect, to the days of evangelical hegemony in the emerging American scientific culture and still look forward to a time when true science and true Christianity will be compellingly synthesized. The Kuyperians, on the other hand, are frankly more pluralistic in their view of the human scientific community. Their outlook is thus suited to those aspects of the evangelical psyche that see evangelicalism as a minority view in a pluralistic society. Much of the confusion in understanding what popular evangelicals and fundamentalists want vis-à-vis American society today stems from the lack of resolution among evangelicals (and fundamentalists) of these intellectual issues. Do they want to dominate the scientific culture or simply be recognized as one voice, as legitimately intellectual as the next?

Each side in this debate, however, is working at reconciling two of the central forces in the American cultural heritage, evangelicalism and modern science. These grew up together with the culture itself and hence will be much more difficult to keep separated than has commonly been assumed.

6. Why Creation Science?

IN THE UNITED STATES during the past century "evolution" has symbolized some of the nation's most bitter religious and cultural conflicts. In a widely held view that perhaps is gaining in popularity, biological evolution is regarded as an opposite of divine creation and hence incompatible with traditional Christian belief. So widespread is this belief that in 1981 the so-called "creationist" movement persuaded two state legislatures to adopt laws that purport to ensure "balanced treatment" of the subject of origins in public schools by countering any treatment of "evolution science" with equal treatment of "creation science."[1] The very appropriation of the name "creationist" for the movement that promotes such legislation reflects a belief in, and even an insistence on, the absolute antithesis between faith in a Creator and biological evolution. In fact the creation-science movement does not advocate creationism in the general sense of any belief in a Divine Creator or even in the more limited sense of belief in creation by the God of Scripture; rather it defends only one view of

1. Act 590 of 1981, State of Arkansas, 73rd General Assembly, Regular Session, 1981. Cf. a similar Louisiana law of 1981. The Arkansas law was declared unconstitutional in Federal District Court. The Louisiana law was struck down by the U.S. Supreme Court.

creation, that based on a literal reading of the first chapters of Genesis.[2] In this view, the six days of creation are literal twenty-four-hour days so that the earth can not be more than some thousands of years old. Evolution of any species, accordingly, is absolutely precluded. So in response to suggestions that there are many other creationist positions that allow for an older earth and for the possibility of at least some evolution, the typical response is "creation scientists maintain that there are only two basic explanations—creation and evolution—all explanations can be included within one or the other of these two basic positions."[3]

This insistence that there are only two polarized positions contradicts the facts concerning the views of Christians and other believers on the relation of creation to evolution. Even among American evangelical Protestants alone, to say nothing of liberal Protestants, varieties of Catholics, Jews, Mormons, Moslems, and so forth, there long have been distinguished advocates of mediating positions, usually designated "theistic evolution" or "progressive creation." Immediately upon the announcement of Darwin's theory some conservative Bible-believers had a ready answer to the suggestion that evolutionary doctrine must undermine faith in a Creator. God controls all natural processes through his providential care. The questions raised by biological evolution are therefore not in principle different from those suggested by other natural phenomena, such as photosynthesis. A fully naturalistic account of the process does not preclude belief that God planned or controlled it. So God may have used evolutionary processes as his means of creating at least some of earth's species. Whether the creation of humans involved some special divine intervention

2. Duane Gish, one of the leaders of the creation-science movement, simply defines creation as "the bringing into being of the basic kinds of plants and animals by the process of sudden, or fiat, creation described in the first two chapters of Genesis"; *Evolution: The Fossils Say No!* (San Diego: Creation-Life Publishers, 1973), p. 24.
3. "ICR Scientist at Westminster College," *Acts & Facts* 119 (May 1983), 4.

has been a matter of some debate among evangelical theistic evolutionists. A strict reading of Genesis, they agreed, however, does not preclude evolutionary developments. After all, already by the mid-nineteenth century most American evangelical scholars concurred that the "days" of Genesis 1 could mean long eras sufficient to allow for the enormous amounts of time demanded by geological theories. Evolutionary doctrine as such, therefore, need contradict neither any theological dogma nor a faithful reading of Scripture.

Such mediating views have a distinguished heritage within American evangelicalism itself. Asa Gray, America's first great proponent of Darwinism, remained an orthodox Congregationalist even though teaching at Unitarian Harvard. He argued in correspondence with Darwin that nothing in the new biological theories entailed lack of divine planning and hence guidance of the processes (unlike Darwin, Calvinists were not distressed by the idea of a God who permitted considerable cruelty and wastefulness in his universe). Gray's protégé and closest collaborator in demonstrating the compatibilities of biological evolution and orthodox belief was George Frederick Wright. Wright's orthodox evangelical credentials were so impeccable that he was asked to contribute an essay on evolution to *The Fundamentals* (1910-1915), the publications that signaled the rise of organized fundamentalism. While criticizing extravagant philosophical and scientific claims of evolution, Wright insisted that the Bible "teaches a system of evolution" and that any demonstrated evolutionary developments would illustrate how God had designed life so to evolve. In fact, Wright held, to believe that all development of species

4. These developments are discussed in many places. The history of Christian discussion of the age of the earth is summarized by Davis A. Young, *Christianity and the Age of the Earth* (Grand Rapids: Zondervan, 1982), pp. 13-67. James R. Moore, *The Post-Darwinian Controversies: A Study of the Protestant Struggle to Come to Terms with Darwin in Great Britain and America 1870-1900* (Cambridge: Cambridge University Press, 1979), presents an impressive account of orthodox Protestant theologians' reconciliations with Darwinism during this period.

happened merely by chance without divine guidance and even intervention was "to commit logical 'hara-kiri.' "[5]

Equally striking are the statements made at about the same time by Benjamin B. Warfield of Princeton Theological Seminary. Warfield, a formidable intellect, was an inventor of the term "inerrancy" and a leading proponent of that key fundamentalist doctrine that Scripture did not err in any of its assertions. Despite such conservativism, Warfield made a point of observing that evolution and creation were not opposites. The discussion, he said, "can never sink again into rest until it is thoroughly understood in all quarters that 'evolution' cannot act as a substitute for creation, but at best can supply only a theory of the method of divine providence."[6] Warfield was clear on the distinctions. Creation might entail supernaturalism; but evolution did not therefore entail antisupernaturalism.

The historical question we are faced with then is why, even when such illustrious leaders of the early fundamentalist movement pointed out the viability of mediating positions, did opposition to all biological evolution become for so many a test of the faith? The mediating positions have, of course, survived and even are dominant among evangelical academics who are heirs to the fundamentalist movement.[7] Nonetheless in the

5. Moore, *Post-Darwinian Controversies,* pp. 269-80; George Frederick Wright, "The Passing of Evolution," *The Fundamentals,* VII (Chicago: Testimony Publishing Company, c. 1912), 5-16.

6. Benjamin B. Warfield, "On the Antiquity and the Unity of the Human Race," *Studies in Theology* (New York: Oxford University Press, 1932), p. 235. Cf. Warfield, "Calvin's Doctrine of the Creation," *Calvin and Calvinism* (New York: Oxford University Press, 1931), p. 31, where he goes out of his way to point out that "Calvin's doctrine of creation is, . . . for all except the souls of men, an evolutionary one."

7. By the 1970s most evangelical scientists teaching at Christian colleges accepted some form of theistic evolution or "progressive creationism," as they often preferred to call it: *Christianity Today* 21 (17 June 1977), 8. This view was advocated by most of the members of the evangelical American Scientific Affiliation: Ronald M. Numbers, "The Dilemma of Evangelical Scientists," in George Marsden, ed., *Evangelicalism and Modern America* (Grand Rapids: Eerdmans, 1984), p. 159. Roland Mushat Frye, "So-Called 'Creation-Science' and Mainstream Christian

current American discussions these positions are either widely ignored or unknown. Not only does the surprisingly influential creation-science movement claim that theistic evolution is literally of the Devil,[8] but whole state legislatures have also adopted the "balanced treatment" laws that assume that creation and evolution are opposites and the only two views worth considering. Certainly the popular press has done little to dispel this impression of a life-or-death struggle for survival of two wholly irreconcilable views.[9] The historical issue I propose to explore is twofold. Why have creation scientists insisted on this polarization, and why have such dichotomized views been so popular in America?

THE ROLE OF THE BIBLE

Central to the rejections of evolution as incompatible with the Christian faith in creation is the belief that "the Bible tells me

---

Rejections," *Proceedings of the American Philosophical Society* 127/1 (January 1983), 61-70, documents some mainline views.

8. For example, Henry M. Morris, "The Spirit of Compromise," *Studies in the Bible and Science or Christ and Creation* (Philadelphia: Presbyterian and Reformed, 1966 [1963]), says "the idea of an evolutionary origin must have had its first beginnings in the mind of Satan himself" (p. 98). Theistic evolution is accordingly precluded (p. 196). Cf. "The Bible and Theistic Evolution" (ibid., pp. 89-93). Among other things, Morris thinks God would not have invented a system involving the extermination of the weak and unfit (p. 92). He also suggests that "it seems incomprehensible that He would waste billions of years in aimless evolutionary meandering before getting to the point"; Henry M. Morris, ed., *Scientific Creationism* (General Edition, San Diego: Creation-Life Publishers, 1974), p. 219. Darwin himself objected to theistic evolution on similar grounds (see note 4 above). The views of Darwin and Morris both reflect post-Calvinist conceptions of what God must be like.

9. Even *Christianity Today*, a journal close to the "progressive creationist" camp, published a major story about the Arkansas trial that included no intimation that there were such mediating positions: Jack Weatherly, "Creationists Concerned about Court Test of Arkansas Law," *Christianity Today* 25 (September 1981), 40-41. Both before and since, the magazine has run articles with more nuanced views.

so." Henry Morris, founder of the most prominent of the current creation-science organizations, says directly that "if man wishes to know anything at all about Creation . . . his sole source of true information is that of divine revelation. . . . This is our textbook on the science of Creation!"[10] In the 1980s court cases this theme was obscured to avert constitutional difficulties. Nonetheless, Morris, his close followers, and his many pious admirers agree that it is obvious that Genesis 1 refers to twenty-four-hour days of creation and so absolutely precludes evolution. One question is, then, why do such principles of biblical interpretation persist with such strength in America? First we must consider the convergence of two powerful traditions of biblical interpretation in America. These, in turn, lead to a number of factors in the American religious and cultural heritage that have inclined some substantial groups of people toward accepting such views.

MILLENARIANISM

The modern premillennial views that have flourished in America since the nineteenth century have often been based on exact interpretations of the numbers in biblical prophecies. The Bible, such millenarians assume, is susceptible to exact scientific analysis, on the basis of which at least some aspects of the future can be predicted with some exactitude. Seventh-Day Adventists, Jehovah's Witnesses, and the influential dispensational premillennialists among fundamentalists all treat the prophetic numbers in this way. For such groups it is accordingly important to have a biblical hermeneutic that will yield exact conclusions. Moreover, the hermeneutical principle that applies to prophecy ought to be consistent with those applied to scriptural reports of past events. Dispensationalists have often used the formula "literal where possible" to describe this

10. Morris, "The Bible *Is* a Textbook of Science" (1964-1965), *Studies in the Bible and Science,* p. 114.

hermeneutic. While they do not wish to apply literal interpretations to statements obviously poetical or figurative ("the
mountains shall clap their hands") they do think that, unless
we are compelled otherwise, we should interpret Scripture as
referring to literal historical events that are being described
exactly. It is not surprising, therefore, that such groups who
derive some of their key doctrines from exact interpretations
of prophecy should be most adamant in interpreting Genesis
1 as describing an exact order of creation in six twenty-four-
hour days. Fundamentalists, often with dispensationalist ties,
have been among the most ardent supporters of the recent
"creation-science" movement that insists on a young earth, and
hence on an entirely antievolutionary view of creation.

The influence of these prophetic views goes beyond the
bounds of their immediate fundamentalist constituents, as is
suggested by the fact that the dispensationalist prophetic
volume by Hal Lindsey, *The Late Great Planet Earth,* was the
best-selling book in America during the 1970s.[11] The principal
creation-science organization, the Institute for Creation Research in San Diego, has close ties to this prophetic movement.
Henry Morris, its founder, for instance, is author of a "literalist" commentary on the book of Revelation.[12] George
McCready Price (1870-1963), the main precursor of Morris's
young-earth flood-geology approaches, was a Seventh-Day Adventist. Price's whole career was dedicated to confirming the
prophecies of Ellen G. White, who claimed divine inspiration
for the view that the worldwide flood accounts for the geological evidence on which geologists built their theories.[13]

11. Grand Rapids: Zondervan, 1970.
12. Henry Morris, *The Revelation Record: A Devotional Commentary on
the Prophetic Book on the End Times,* forewords by Tim LaHaye and Jerry
Falwell (Wheaton, IL: Tyndale House, 1983). Such views on prophecy are
not, however, the official views of the Institute for Christian Research;
Henry Morris, ICR letter, February 1983.
13. Ronald L. Numbers, "Creationism in 20th-Century America,"
Science 218 (5 November 1982), 539. Numbers, here and elsewhere, has
done valuable work in documenting the rise of creation-science organizations and ideas.

PROTESTANT SCHOLASTICISM

Not all creation-scientists are millenarians, however. Another formidable tradition in American Protestantism that often has supported interpretations of Genesis 1 and has influenced both American fundamentalism and popular American conceptions of Scripture is Protestant scholasticism. This tradition has been articulated most prominently by the Princeton theologians, such as Benjamin Warfield, who popularized the concept of the "inerrancy" of Scripture. The Princetonians, however, were by no means the inventors of this concept nor the only major purveyors of it in America. The substance of the inerrancy view—that because the Bible is God's Word it must be accurate in matters of science and history as well as in doctrine—was already held in much of the scholastic Protestantism of the seventeenth century and was common in many quarters of nineteenth-century American Protestantism.[14] Belief in the inerrancy of Scripture did not entail that it always be interpreted as literally as possible, as demonstrated by the allowance for long "days" of creation by most Princetonians and the allowance for limited biological evolution by Warfield himself. Nonetheless, for some who adopted the Princetonian formulations on Scripture the emphasis on scientific exactness of scriptural statements was conducive to views of those who insisted that Genesis 1 referred to literal twenty-four days.

A less ambiguous conservatism is found in the Lutheran Church—Missouri Synod. For reasons no doubt related both to their Protestant scholastic tradition and to determination to resist infection by modern American theologies, the leading

14. John Woodbridge, *Biblical Authority: A Critique of the Rogers/McKim Proposal* (Grand Rapids: Zondervan, 1982), by collecting counterinstances, counterbalances suggestions that the concept originated in the late nineteenth century. Ian Rennie, "An Historical Response to Jack Rogers" (Unpublished paper, 1981), clarifies the development of emphasis on something like "inerrancy" that seems to have received emphasis among some Protestants primarily since the seventeenth century.

Missouri Synod theologians in the first half of the twentieth century insisted on a view of Scripture perhaps even more conservative than that of the Princeton theologians. In their view the Holy Spirit dictated or suggested to the writers the very words of Scripture. God therefore is properly the author of Scripture. Moreover, the words of Scripture have divine properties,[15] according to the Missouri Synod interpreters. These considerations led to the conclusion that the days of Genesis 1 were twenty-four-hour periods, a point they insisted on. This conclusion, they said, was necessitated by the words of Scripture itself (such as referring to the "evening and the morning" of the days). Evolution, accordingly, was necessarily "atheistic and immoral" and theistic evolution inconsistent with both Scripture and true evolution.[16] Missouri Synod spokesmen argued that evolution itself was unscientific and a threat to civilization and to church doctrine.[17] No doubt the general cultural conservatism and defensiveness in the Missouri Synod contributed to a conservative hermeneutic that precluded all evolution. The central argument, however, was the appeal to Scripture itself. In any case, when Henry Morris first organized the Creation Research Society in 1963, out of which grew most recent creation science, one-third of the original steering committee were Missouri Synod Lutherans.[18]

---

15. John Mueller, based on lectures of Francis Pieper, *Christian Dogmatics* (St. Louis: Concordia, 1934), pp. 104 and 120. Benjamin Warfield says: " . . . this conception of co-authorship implies that the Spirit's superintendence extends to the choice of the words by the human authors (verbal inspiration), and preserves its product from everything inconsistent with a divine authorship . . . thus securing, among other things, that entire truthfulness which is everywhere presupposed in and asserted for Scripture by the biblical writers (inerrancy)"; "The Real Problem of Inspiration," in Samuel Craig, ed., *The Inspiration and Authority of the Bible* (Philadelphia: Presbyterian and Reformed Publishing Company, 1948), p. 173.

16. Ibid., p. 181. Cf. Theodore Graebner, *Essays on Evolution* (St. Louis: Concordia, 1925).

17. Cf. Graebner, *Essays*, pp. 16 and passim.

18. Numbers, "Creationism," p. 542.

RATIONAL AND SCIENTIFIC CHRISTIANITY

Common to the prophetic-millennial and the scholastic traditions and relating them to each other has been a desire to
establish a firm rational basis for Christian belief. Both traditions have emphasized conventional proofs for the existence
of God and the truth of Christianity.[19] Since the seventeenth
century many Christian apologists have considered it important to demonstrate that Christianity is a properly scientific
belief. Especially in the eighteenth and the nineteenth centuries, defenders of Christianity assiduously collected evidences
from natural sciences to confirm truths revealed in Scripture.
Nineteenth-century American apologists, whether scholastic
or millenarian, typically based their apologetics on explicitly
Baconian principles. They insisted that their arguments were
based on cautious examination of evidence that everyone
could observe through commonsense procedures. Speculative
hypotheses would be avoided, so that arguments would be
limited to careful induction. Evidences either from the physical sciences or evidences analogous to those in the physical
sciences were preferred. The book of nature and the book of
Scripture were fully harmonious and to be understood, as
Bishop Butler had so persuasively argued, in analogous
ways.[20]

Crucial to the creation-science movement is the desire
to restore this harmony of science and Scripture which the
twentieth-century intellectual climate seemingly had shat-
tered. In the wake of the derision heaped upon William Jen-

19. For example, Theodore Graebner, *God and the Cosmos: A Critical
Analysis of Atheism* (Grand Rapids: Eerdmans, 1932), esp. pp. 31-36;
Charles Hodge, *Systematic Theology,* I (New York: Scribner's, 1871); Ar-
thur T. Pierson, *Many Infallible Proofs: The Evidences of Christianity* (New
York: Revell, 1886).

20. Two helpful evaluations of the assumption that the evidences
for the truths of Scripture will be similar to the evidences for natural
science are Roland Mushat Frye, "Metaphors, Equations, and the Faith,"
Theology Today, April 1980, pp. 59-67; and Langdon Gilkey, "Creationism:
The Roots of the Conflict," *Christianity and Crisis,* 26 April 1982, pp. 108-15.

nings Bryan and fundamentalists generally after the Scopes
trial, some literal-minded Bible believers set out to demonstrate that, contrary to popular opinion, science still supported Scripture. Henry Morris made this point explicitly in
his first book, *That You Might Believe* (1946). While acknowl-
edging that Christian truths must ultimately be based on faith
and that he would accept the Bible "even against reason if
need be," Morris emphasized that the Bible "in no way does
violence to common sense and intelligence." The twentieth-
century problem was that many people regarded Christianity
"as outmoded beliefs, conceived in superstition and nurtured
by scientific and philosophical illiteracy." Morris, by contrast,
was sure that biblical beliefs would satisfy even his engineer's
habit "of requiring satisfactory evidence and proof of all that
they accept as fact."[21]

Buoyed by this confidence in the Bible, Morris proceeded
to illustrate "the great number of scientific truths that have
lain hidden within its pages for thirty centuries or more, only
to be discovered by man's enterprise within the last few centuries or even years." These facts included evidences such as
that the stars "cannot be numbered," or that the psalms directly
described evaporation, wind, and electrical discharges as the
cause of rain (Psalm 135:7). "He causeth the vapor to ascend
from the ends of the earth; He maketh lightnings for the rain;
He bringeth the wind out of His treasuries." The creation-
science movement grew out of this impulse. While not claiming
actually to prove that Christianity must be true, it seeks decisive
evidences confirming biblical statement. So, not only do creation scientists assemble scientific evidences pointing to a
worldwide flood, they sponsor expeditions searching for
Noah's Ark.

The whole enterprise relates to a distinctive view of Scripture itself. Fundamentalists and their allies regard the Bible as
filled with scientific statements of the same precision as might

21. Henry M. Morris, *That You Might Believe* (Chicago: Good Books,
Inc., 1946), p. 4.

be found in twentieth-century scientific journals.[22] God, they assume, would not reveal himself any less accurately. In the seminal *Genesis Flood,* Morris and John C. Whitcomb affirm "the complete divine inspiration and perspicuity of Scripture, believing that a true exegesis thereof yields determinative Truth in all matters with which it deals."[23] By "Truth," they mean the scientifically accurate facts that Scripture contains. In the fundamentalist and the scholastic traditions the Bible is regarded as a book of "facts." So Charles Hodge in an often-quoted statement observed, "If natural science be concerned with the facts and laws of nature, theology is concerned with the facts and the principles of the Bible."[24]

In such traditions, the principal goal of biblical study was to classify the facts in Baconian fashion. "The methods of modern science are applied to Bible study," said dispensationalist spokesman Reuben Torrey, "thorough analysis followed by careful synthesis."[25]

Perhaps most importantly, this assumption that Scripture speaks with scientific accuracy has invited the literalist hermeneutic that allows scriptural language as few ambiguities as possible. For instance, one of the most common arguments against evolution of species is that Genesis 1 repeatedly says that plants and animals should produce "after their kind." This phrase is usually regarded as precluding one species ever producing another. Similarly, a well-known dispensationalist argues

22. As Eileen Barker observes, "Those rejecting the values and consequences of a scientific world view are nonetheless children of the age of science"; "In the Beginning: The Battle of Creationist Science against Evolutionism," in Roy Wallis, ed., *On the Margins of Science: The Social Construction of Rejected Knowledge,* Sociological Review Monograph 27 (Keele, Eng.: University of Keele, 1979), 183.

23. John C. Whitcomb and Henry M. Morris, *The Genesis Flood: The Biblical Record and its Scientific Implications* (Grand Rapids: Baker Book House, 1981 [1961]), p. xx. They also quote approvingly the Warfield passage cited above (note 15).

24 Hodge, *Systematic Theology,* I, 18.

25. Reuben Torrey, *What the Bible Teaches,* 17th ed. (New York: Revell, 1933 [1898]), p. 1.

against any compatibility of evolution and the Bible by quoting
Genesis 2:7, which states that man was created "out of the dust
of the ground." But why, he asks, can this not allow a gradual
evolution from the primordial dust? "This could not refer to or
include a former animal ancestry, since it is to dust that man
returns—and this is not a return to an animal state (Gen. 3:19)."
Neither will this author allow that the first chapters of Genesis
might be allegories that "still retain the 'thrust' of the Bible."
Such a solution would dishonor God because, if evolution were
true, the allegory would be "an entirely inaccurate one" so that
"in giving it God was either untrue or unintelligent."[26] Even
allegory, in this view, has to point directly toward the literal facts.

COMMON SENSE

Scholars from other traditions might find such thinking incredible and surely to involve applying linguistic standards of
one age to another. Nonetheless, there can be no doubt that
in our age such thinking is widely regarded as common sense.
Fundamentalists and kindred religious movements have made
strong claims to stand for common sense. Such popular appeals reflect the nineteenth-century American evangelical heritage where Scottish commonsense realism was long the most
influential philosophy.[27]

The Bible, according to the democratic popularization
of this view, is best interpreted by the naïve readings that
common people today give it. "In ninety-nine out of a
hundred cases," wrote Reuben Torrey, "the meaning that the
plain man gets out of the Bible is the correct one."[28] In

26. Charles C. Ryrie, "The Bible and Evolution," *Bibliotheca Sacra*
124 (1967), 66 and 67.
27. Cf. George M. Marsden, *Fundamentalism and American Culture:
The Shaping of Twentieth-Century Evangelicalism, 1870-1925* (New York: Oxford University Press, 1980), esp. pp. 15-16, 55-62, 215-21.
28. Quoted in William G. McLoughlin, Jr., *Modern Revivalism* (New
York: Ronald Press, 1959), p. 372. Original source not clear, from 1906.

modern America common sense is infused with popular conceptions of straightforward empirical representations of what is really "out there." Mystical, metaphorical, and symbolical perceptions of reality have largely disappeared. Instead, most Americans share what sociologist Michael Cavanaugh designates an "empiricist folk epistemology."[29] Things are thought best described exactly the way they appear, accurately with no hidden meanings. Such folk epistemology, it happens, is close to that which works best for engineers—straightforward, consistent, factual, with no nonsense. In fact, there are an unusual number of engineers in the creation-science movement.[30] Henry Morris, an engineer himself, connects his engineering standards to his standards for biblical hermeneutics. "Probably for no class of people more than engineers do common sense and reason have their greatest value, and I hope that these qualities have not remained completely undeveloped in me."[31] Many of his readers will agree, Morris correctly observes, that such "common sense and reason" must be applied to biblical interpretation.

Most contemporary scientists have difficulty understanding the degree to which the alleged scientific arguments of creation science also appeal to popular common sense. Evolution may have scientific experts on its side, but it simply

---

Cf. William B. Riley, "The Faith of the Fundamentalists," *Current History* 26 (June 1927), 434-36, reprinted in Willard B. Gatewood, Jr., ed., *Controversy in the Twenties: Fundamentalism, Modernism, and Evolution* (Nashville: Vanderbilt University Press, 1969), who says, "Fundamentalism insists upon the plain intent of scripture-speech. . . ." This "scientific" approach he contrasts with the liberal "weasel method" of interpretation (pp. 75 and 76).

29. This phrase is suggested to me by Michael A. Cavanaugh, "Science, True Science, Pseudoscience: The One-eyed Religious Movement for Scientific Creationism," draft of unpublished manuscript, 13 September 1982, p. 17. Cavanaugh's completed work is "A Sociological Account of Scientific Creationism: Science, True Science, Pseudoscience" (Ph.D. dissertation, University of Pittsburgh, 1983).

30 Dorthy Nelkin, *The Creation Controversy: Science or Scripture in the Schools* (New York: Norton, 1982), pp. 70-90.

31. Morris, *That You Might Believe*, p. 4.

strains popular common sense. It is simply difficult to believe that the amazing order of life on earth arose spontaneously out of the original disorder of the universe. Perhaps a common sense deeper than any culturally conditioned beliefs invites people who look at "the starry skies above and the moral law within" to believe that a personality, rather than blind chance, must have arranged these. The development of specific mechanisms, such as the eye, through blind chance also stretches common credulity. Could everything appear so ordered just by accident? The odds against a monkey at the typewriter producing an organized sentence by random typing is a favorite example. The length of time it would take for the present order of life to arise from disorder is staggering and stretches popular conceptions of probability.[32] As a commonsense argument, an antisupernaturalistic evolutionary outlook is far less compelling than the old argument from design.

As to the fact that so many experts agree on the truth of evolution, experts have often been wrong. Besides, the experts contradict one another, so the layperson has no obligation to believe them. Creation scientists, moreover, can produce their own experts, as creation-science organizations emphasize. In addition, however, people should be "deciding for themselves in a reasonable way." Audiences in church basements are told to go "see for themselves" fossil evidence that supposedly undermines evolution. "Let's decide upon a method by which we can resolve the controversy," says a typical appeal, "set up definitions, then examine the evidences."[33]

The American folk epistemology, then, is by no means antiscientific in principle. Rather it is based on a naïve realism plus popular mythology concerning proper scientific procedure and verification. These procedures are essentially Ba-

---

32. Cf. the arguments of Duane T. Gish, "It is Either 'In the Beginning, God'—or ' . . . Hydrogen,'" *Christianity Today* 26 (8 October 1982), 28-33.

33. R. L. Wysong, *Creation—The Evolution Controversy: Toward a Rational Solution* (Midland, MI: Inquiry Press, 1976), pp. 17 and 29.

conian, favoring simple empirical evidence.[34] The view of science is essentially optimistic and progressive; true science will eventually reach the truth, though it may be led off the track by prejudice. Neither are true science and Christianity in any conflict. True science can and will confirm Christian revelation. Michael Cavanaugh has suggested the marvelous characterization for this widespread American demand for empirical support of the faith as "doubting Thomism."[35]

THE SENSE OF CULTURAL CRISIS—THE SOUTH AFTER THE CIVIL WAR

The popular appeal of uncompromising antievolutionists results not only from the coincidence of their hermeneutical and apologetic assumptions with much of American folk epistemology but also from their ability to convince their followers that antievolution is crucial to the future of civilization. Militant antievolutionists are almost all Northern European Protestants. Many of them have emphasized vigorously America's Christian (Protestant) heritage.[36] A sense of cultural crisis, typically described as a turning from Christian to secular civilization, seems an important factor in raising the stakes of the antievolution effort and hence reducing the likelihood of compromise.

This combination of beliefs seems more characteristic of the United States than of other countries[37] and more charac-

34. Cf. Marsden, *Fundamentalism*, pp. 55-62, 215-21.

35. Cavanaugh, "Science, True Science . . . ," draft of 21 February 1983, passim. Another felicitous phrase from Cavanaugh is "the epistemic priesthood of all believers," draft of 13 September 1982, p. 21.

36. Christian Heritage College, where patriotic evangelist Tim LaHaye is a leading figure, has close links with the Institute for Creation Research. Creation science is promoted by the Moral Majority (in which LaHaye is also active). Missouri Synod Lutherans perhaps are an exception, showing less concern for the Christian American ideal.

37. Cf. George M. Marsden, "Fundamentalism as an American Phenomenon, A Comparison with English Evangelicalism," *Church History*

teristic of the South than of the rest of the nation. Antievolution legislation and the recent creation laws have far better records in the states of the former Confederacy than elsewhere in the nation. Moreover, the irreconcilability of evolution and the Bible is a widely popular belief in the South not resting on the specific arguments or organizations of the recent creation-science movement, but antedating these.[38] It seems then that one clue to understanding the nature of militant antievolutionism is to look at some circumstances in which evolutionism has become for a substantial group of people identified with cultural decay.

The easy answer to explaining the strength of antievolutionism in the South is the prevalence of the "old-time religion" and relatively low levels of education of many southern Bible-believers.[39] These factors are certainly important, although they do not explain why a particular belief (the dangers of evolution) gained an elevated status in southern folk religion.[40] An interesting question is why antievolution became a standard test of the faith among southern evangelicals earlier than it did among northern fundamentalists.

A brief look at one incident in southern antievolution history—the dismissal of James Woodrow from Columbia Theological Seminary in 1886—is instructive in answering these questions. Although this episode took place among the

---

36/2 (June 1977), 215-32. Eileen Barker, "In the Beginning," in Wallis, ed., *On the Margins of Science*, pp. 179-200, seems to confirm that, although creation science in England is similar to that in the United States, it has much less support and influence.

38. Michael Cavanaugh, "Science, True Science, Pseudoscience," draft of 13 September 1982, p. 32, shows that the actual creation-science movement is not especially strong in the states of Arkansas and Louisiana where creation-science legislation has been adopted. He suggests that the reason for this is that the movement is redundant in those states.

39. Recent polls have confirmed these generalizations. Cf. Corwin Smidt, " 'Born Again' Politics: The Political Attitudes and Behavior of Evangelical Christians in the South" (Unpublished paper, March 1982).

40. A comparison of southern white and black attitudes on the subject might be illuminating.

Presbyterian elite, it nonetheless was paralleled in other southern denominations and received the widest coverage and popularization in the religious press. In the South, where an elite remained influential, the intellectual leadership successfully signaled to their constituency that acceptance of any form of biological evolution was a grave danger to the faith. For the popularizers this was easily translated into the question of whether one's ancestors were monkeys and the evangelists could take over from there. As the *Texas Presbyterian* put it, " 'The Lord formed man of the dust of the ground.' Man was born of an ape by ordinary generation. If these are not logical contraries, it would, in ordinary circumstances, be accounted a very strange use of language."[41]

The case of James Woodrow is a classic instance, arguably *the* classic instance, of the American and southern tendency to draw a false dichotomy between creation and every form of biological evolution. In 1861 Woodrow was appointed to a chair, "Professor of Natural Science in Connexion with Religion," at Columbia Theological Seminary, a leading institution of the Presbyterian Church in the United States (Southern Presbyterian). The establishment of this rather unusual theological chair reflected optimism among some southern theologians as to the positive value of demonstrating the harmonies of science and Scripture. Others, notably the famed Robert L. Dabney, were less ready to concede that the Bible needed any help from the scientific quarter.[42] James Woodrow's stance on science and the Bible involved basically conservative harmonizations, such as between the long "days" of Genesis 1 and the old earth suggested by modern geology. Although he taught about evolutionary views during the first two decades of his tenure at Columbia, he inclined against the theory. Gradually,

41. *Texas Presbyterian,* 19 September 1884, quoted in Ernest Trice Thompson, *Presbyterians in the South,* Vol. 2: *1861-1890* (Richmond: John Knox Press, 1973), p. 466. Cf. p. 477 on the unusually positive reception to antirevolutionary statements in the Southern Presbyterian religious press.

42. Thompson, *Presbyterians,* II, 454.

however, he was swayed by some of the scientific arguments and in 1884 publicly acknowledged his acceptance of a limited form of theistic evolution. Woodrow was, however, a proponent of what had recently become known as the "inerrancy" of Scripture.[43] In fact he was so conservative on the question of the need to harmonize science with the direct statements of Scripture that he held that, while God could have created the body (not the soul) of Adam "mediately" by evolution from the dust of the ground, the body of Eve was created immediately from Adam's rib.

Such literalism was not sufficient to satisfy either the Presbyterian hierarchy or the popular religious press. After a complicated controversy in various Presbyterian judicatories, the General Assembly of the denomination in 1886 finally declared that "Adam and Eve were created, body and soul, by immediate acts of Almighty power," and that Adam's body was created "without any human parentage of any kind," and that any method of biblical interpretation that led to denial of these conclusions would eventually "lead to the denial of doctrines fundamental to the faith."[44] On this basis Woodrow was dismissed from his professorship.[45]

Why did Southern Presbyterians thus try to bolt the door on even the most modest accommodation between creation and evolution? A number of factors converged. First are the dynamics of southern white church and religious life after the Civil War. The war brought the restoration of the Union but not the reunion of the churches. Southern Christians had to justify this continued separation from their former brethren. The most

43. Clement Eaton, "Professor James Woodrow and the Freedom of Teaching in the South," *Journal of Southern History* 28/1 (February 1962), 10.

44. Quoted in Thompson, *Presbyterians*, II, 481.

45. Woodrow, clearly, was personally respected. He also did remain in good standing as a minister in the denomination, an indication that even his opponents recognized that he did not follow his doctrines to their allegedly heretical conclusions. The most complete account of the incident is in Thompson, *Presbyterians*, II, 457-90.

likely principial explanation was that their northern counterparts had been infected by a liberal spirit, evidenced in the first instance in their unbiblical attacks upon slavery. Southern conservatives were thus alert for, and no doubt even eager to notice, any other trends toward laxity in Yankee religion. The continued separation was justified by the mounting conviction in the minds of Southerners that theirs were the only pure representatives of their denominations left. As one church paper declared, "the glory and the strength of our Southern church" is "that there are very few, if any" advocates of change.[46]

Such justifications of separation from the northern churches were an integral part of the southern glorification of the lost cause in the half-century after the War Between the States. Although Southerners had lost the war on the battlefield, they were determined to win the war of ideas.[47] The effect of this determination was to preclude change in any area and to celebrate whatever had been dominant in the antebellum era. This southern determination arose almost simultaneously with the rapid spread of evolutionary ideas at all levels of the rest of Anglo-American thought. So the widespread belief in the value of change became particularly anathema in southern thought. In theology the southern conservatives focused on the issue clearly. As John L. Girardeau, one of the principal opponents of Woodrow put it, "There is a specious and dangerous form of this theory of development of doctrine that threatens, at the present day, to invade the supremacy of the written Word."[48] Moreover, from the perspective of the Southerners' romanticized self-image, evolution, or change of any sort, could be only a decline.

Such circumstances may have been sufficient to ensure some opposition to any evolutionary doctrine at the popular level. In addition, the theologians' stance on the issue of Gene-

46. Quoted in Thompson, *Presbyterians,* II, 447.
47. Charles Reagan Wilson, *Baptized in Blood: The Religion of the Lost Cause* (Athens: University of Georgia Press, 1980).
48. Quoted in Thompson, *Presbyterians,* II, 448.

sis and biological evolution was reinforced by a firm commitment to a scholastic literalist hermeneutic. The Southern Presbyterians had been closely connected with the Old School Presbyterians at Princeton before the war, and so retained the essentials of that conservative-scientific approach to scriptural interpretation. This Presbyterian stance, especially in its Baconian tendencies to view the Bible as a collection of factual propositions, was at one with most biblical interpretation in the South.[49] Perhaps most importantly for the Southerners, however, was that they had been committed both to a literalistic hermeneutic and a nondevelopmentalism by the slavery controversy. The Bible condemned slavery only if one forsook the letter of the text for the alleged spirit. Committed to the letter of Scripture regarding slavery, southern conservatives were hardly in a position to play fast and loose with other passages that might be reinterpreted in the light of alleged modern progress.

FUNDAMENTALISM AFTER WORLD WAR I

The rise of the fundamentalist campaigns against evolution in the 1920s is far better known and need only be summarized here. As we have already seen, outside the South before World War I, antievolution does not appear often to have been a test of the faith, except among sectarians. Probably most conservative Protestants had the impression that evolution and the Bible were irreconcilable opposites, but enough of their leaders saw the problems in this stance to prevent it from becoming a test of fellowship.

As we have seen, even *The Fundamentals* of 1910 to 1915 did not absolutely preclude all evolutionary views. During the 1920s, however, antievolution became increasingly important

49. Cf. E. Brooks Holifield, *The Gentlemen Theologians: American Theology in Southern Culture, 1795-1860* (Durham, NC: Duke University Press, 1978).

to fundamentalists and eventually became an essential hallmark of the true faith.[50]

The rise of the antievolution issue in fundamentalism was related to the convergence of several forces that took their exact shape when precipitated by the catalytic action of the American experience in World War I. The war exacerbated mounting liberal-versus-conservative Protestant tensions, especially as modernists turned on premillennialists for their failure to identify the kingdom with present efforts for the advance of worldwide democracy. Premillennialists and other Protestant conservatives, on the other hand, made the most of the extravagant anti-German propaganda by pointing out that German theology was the source of much modernist thinking. German theology and German "*kultur*," they said, had in common evolutionary philosophies. This "might is right" ideology had led to disaster for that civilization, which had lost all sense of decency. Evolution, moreover, had turned Germans away from faith in the Bible. The same thing that happened to Luther's Germany could happen to Protestant America. When the war ended, some of the American spirit to solve the world's problems through a crusade turned to the home front. For fundamentalists antievolution could serve as an important unifying principle, giving their version of the crusade wide import for civilization itself. The single concept of the threat of evolution explained the connections among the fundamentalist defense of conservative readings of Scripture, their battles to combat modernist theology, and the entire destiny of America.[51]

The campaign needed only a leader to become a national sensation. William Jennings Bryan played that role as no one else could have. In estimating the reasons for the rise of an idea one must not underestimate the role of a charismatic personality. The battle for antievolution, the Bible, and civi-

---

50. Antievolution does not typically appear in the various lists of "fundamentals" drawn up by fundamentalists in the years immediately after World War I.

51. This account is based on Marsden, *Fundamentalism and American Culture*, pp. 141-228.

lization was a cause whose time had come; but it is doubtful that it would have become such a deeply engraved line of American thought had it not been for the colorful leadership of Bryan. If nothing else, Bryan's presence ensured wide press coverage, which of course always invited further simplications of the issue.[52]

Bryan's own understanding of the connection between biological evolution and the dangers of evolutionary philosophies to society was an unusual one. In his view, evolutionary social views led to social Darwinism and hence to anti-Progressive politics and glorification of war. His followers, however, were not especially concerned with the details of the threat of evolution to civilization. They were convinced there was a threat to traditional beliefs posed by the spread of naturalistic, evolutionary-developmental philosophies. This supposition was not entirely fanciful. Bryan and his cohorts were aware in a general way of the same secularizing trends associated with evolutionary naturalism in philosophy that their intellectual contemporaries, such as Carl Becker and Joseph Wood Krutch, were also pointing out.

The beauty of the fundamentalists' position was that they could relate this threat to civilization directly to the abandonment of the Bible as a source of authority and truth. This linkage was most clear concerning the question of biological evolution. Here again, the fundamentalists were pointing to a real phenomenon of major cultural significance. American young people, especially those who were attending colleges, were forsaking traditional faith in the Bible in droves. Bryan was especially impressed by the 1916 study by Bryn Mawr professor James H. Leuba who demonstrated the dramatic erosion of traditional beliefs among American college students

52. Two recent accounts that are helpful on the role of Bryan are Willard H. Smith, *The Social and Religious Thought of William Jennings Bryan* (Lawrence, KS: Coronado Press, 1975); and Ferenc Morton Szasz, *The Divided Mind of Protestant America, 1880-1930* (University, AL: University of Alabama Press, 1982). Szasz argues particularly well for the crucial influence of Bryan.

from their freshmen to their senior years. Science courses, especially those that taught naturalistic evolution, were leading contributors to this revolution. In fact, nearly two-thirds of the nation's biologists professed not to believe in a personal God or in immortality for humans.[53] The teaching of evolution was, then, a real contributor to a trend that many considered to have ominous implications for the future of civilization.

The perception of such stakes invited the sort of polarization of the issue that we have been discussing. Bryan's appeal to quasi-populist rural resentments against experts, especially in the South, added to the oversimplifications. Bryan's own case is especially revealing, since the private Bryan and the public Bryan of the 1920s seem to have disagreed on how simple the issue was. Bryan himself held to a somewhat moderate interpretation of Genesis 1. As Darrow elicited from him at the Scopes trial, Bryan believed that Genesis 1 might allow for an old earth,[54] a belief that was not unusual among fundamentalist leaders.[55] Bryan even confided just before the trial to Howard A. Kelly, a prominent Johns Hopkins physician and one of the contributors to *The Fundamentals*, that he agreed that one need have no objection to "evolution before man."[56] Yet in his public speeches Bryan had been allowing no compromise. "The so-called theistic evolutionists refuse to admit that they are atheists," he argued. Theistic evolution, he added, was just "an anesthetic administered to young Christians to deaden the pain while their

53. James R. Moore, *The Post-Darwinian Controversies*, p. 73.

54. *The World's Most Famous Court Trial: State of Tennessee v. John Thomas Scopes: Complete Stenographic Report* (New York, 1971; Cincinnati, 1925), p. 302. Bryan admits that he thinks the "days" of Genesis 1 are long periods and observes, "I think it would be just as easy for the kind of God we believe in to make the earth in six days or six years or in 6,000,000 years or in 600,000,000 years."

55. Cf. *A Debate: Resolved That the Creative Days in Genesis Were Aeons, Not Solar Days*, William B. Riley for the affirmative, Harry Rimmer for the negative (Duluth: Research Science Bureau, n.d., c. 1920s). Riley was president of the World's Christian Fundamentals Association.

56. Numbers, "Creationism," p. 540.

religion is being removed by the materialists."[57] Bryan explained this inconsistency of his stances in his letter to Kelly: "A concession as to the truth of evolution up to man furnishes our opponents with an argument which they are quick to use, namely, if evolution accounts for all the species up to man, does it not raise a presumption in behalf of evolution to include man?"[58] The impact of a skilled popular leader in polarizing issues is evident here. Convinced that the issues were of unparalleled importance, Bryan was not going to allow his constituency to be distracted from the warfare by the fine distinctions of mediating positions.

THE WARFARE METAPHOR

Exacerbating the tendencies to polarization, arising from the convergence of all the above factors, has been the sheer power of military metaphors. For over a century warfare has been the dominant popular image for considering the relationships between science and religion, evolution and creation. Journalists, and historians only somewhat less, relish reporting a good fight. Reports that there is a war, moreover, can help ensure that hostilities continue.

In the historiography of the relationship between Darwinism and religion, argues James R. Moore in the most extensive treatment of this theme, the military metaphor was first promoted by the opponents of religion. In fact, ever since the famed Bishop Wilberforce–T. H. Huxley encounter of 1860, there was something of a warfare between churchmen and antisupernaturalist Darwinists. Given the many suggestions that the two outlooks might be reconciled, however, these conflicts might easily have been resolved or confined. Militant opponents of the whole Christian cultural and intellectual es-

57. Bryan, "Darwinism in Public Schools," *The Commoner,* January 1923, pp. 1 and 2.
58. Numbers, "Creationism," p. 540.

tablishment, however, made the most of the conflict. Darwin's personal difficulties in seeing how theism could fit with his theories lent aid to their cause. Accordingly, Victorian polemicists like T. H. Huxley and historians such as John William Draper and Andrew Dickson White reinforced the idea that the whole history of the relations between science and religion was a "warfare."[59] As the statistics on the low number of traditional theists among early twentieth-century American biologists show, the weapon of Darwinism was indeed taking a heavy toll in this warfare on Christianity.

Given this actual hostility of many Darwinists toward traditional Christianity, it is not surprising that some Christian groups replied in kind. Particularly this was true of groups that already saw most of reality through warfare imagery. Sects are notorious on this score. Immigrant groups and Southerners each had their own reasons to view themselves as at least being in a cold war with the surrounding culture. Anti-evolution hostilities, however, did not reach nationwide proportions until the rise of fundamentalism in the 1920s. Fundamentalism was a peculiar blend of sectarianism and aspirations to dominate the culture. A coalition of conservative Protestant traditions, its most conspicuous unifying feature has been militancy. As Richard Hofstadter observes, "The fundamentalist mind . . . is essentially Manichean; it looks upon the world as an arena for conflict between absolute good and absolute evil, and accordingly it scorns compromises (who can compromise with Satan?)." William Jennings Bryan's refusal to admit publicly the possibility of limited evolution for fear of giving a weapon to the enemy illustrates this tendency. In later fundamentalism, which has provided most of the leadership for the recent creation-science movement, compromises have been even less welcomed. The 1981 Arkansas creation-science law, for instance, in requiring the teaching of "a relatively recent inception of the Earth and of living kinds" to counterbalance antisupernaturalistic "evolution-science" would have

59. Moore, *Post-Darwinian Controversies*, pp. 19-49.

excluded Bryan's own position that the "days" of Genesis could represent aeons.[60]

THE MYTHOLOGICAL POWERS OF
EVOLUTIONARY EXPLANATION

William Allen White said of Bryan that he was never wrong in political diagnosis and never right in prescription.[61] We might say the same thing of the creation-science movement that has been heir to his work. They have correctly identified some important trends in twentieth-century American life and see that these trends have profound cultural implications. Basically, they point to the revolution that has brought the wide dominance in American academia and much other public life of antisupernaturalistic relativism. Evolutionary theory has been, as we have seen, often used to support such an outlook. Carl Sagan's immensely popular *Cosmos* furnished a telling example. "The cosmos is all there is, there was, or ever will be," he states in his opening sentence.[62]

Such views are, of course, philosophical premises rather than conclusions of scientific inquiry, since no conceivable amount of scientific evidence could settle such an issue. Nonetheless, the fundamentalists of both sides make the same mistake in debating such questions. Both fundamentalistic antisupernaturalists, such as Sagan, and their creation-scientist

60. Richard Hofstadter, *Anti-Intellectualism in American Life* (New York: Vintage Books, 1962), p. 135. Act 590 of 1981, State of Arkansas, 73rd General Assembly Regular Session, 1981, section 4. Creationists indicate that "relatively recent inception" means from 6,000 to 20,000 years ago. Judge William R. Overton, in the United States District Court, Eastern District of Arkansas Western Division Judgment, Rev. Bill McLean, et al., vs. The Arkansas Board of Education, et al., 5 January 1982, p. 24.

61. Szasz, *Divided Mind*, pp. 122-23.

62. Carl Sagan, *Cosmos* (New York: Random House, 1980), p. 4. Cf. R. C. Lewontin, "Darwin's Revolution," *New York Review of Books* 30/10 (16 June 1983), 22, who insists that "Science cannot coexist" with "an all-powerful God who at any moment can disrupt natural relations."

opponents approach the issue as though it could be settled on the grounds of some scientific evidence. In each case, the oversimplification of the issue reflects widespread overestimation in American culture of the possible range of scientific inquiry.

Beyond such overestimation of the prowess of science in general is the peculiar role that "evolution" has come to play in the antisupernaturalist cultural and intellectual revolution. Both antisupernaturalists and their creation-scientist opponents have reflected common parlance when they have spoken of "evolutionary science" as equivalent to "naturalism"—that is, a view that the universe is controlled by natural forces insusceptible to influence by an ultimately supernatural plan or guidance.

Moreover, it seems correct to argue, as does David N. Livingstone, that evolution has become an all-explanatory metaphor in modern culture. It has become, Livingstone suggests, a "cosmic myth—a worldview which purports to provide, for example, guidelines for ethics and a coherent account of reality." All aspects of being and experience are explained according to evolutionary, developmental, or historicist models. Often these are presented as complete accounts of the phenomena involved or as the only meaningful accounts that humans have available. Evolution is, of course, a model with valuable explanatory powers; but it is worth asking, as Livingstone does, whether we have any adequate basis for making this metaphor the foundation for an all-comprehensive worldview.[63] In any case, creation scientists are correct in perceiving that in modern culture "evolution" often involves far more than biology. The basic ideologies of the civilization, including its entire moral structure, are at stake. Evolution does sometimes function as a mythological system, sometimes as the key element in a worldview that functions as a virtual religion. Given this actual connection

63. David N. Livingstone, "Evolution as Myth and Metaphor," *Christian Scholar's Review* 12/2 (1983), 111-25, quotation from p. 119.

with a philosophy antithetical to traditional Christianity, it is all the more difficult for many to see that the biological theory is not *necessarily* connected with such a worldview. Dogmatic proponents of evolutionary antisupernaturalistic mythologies have been inviting responses in kind.

7. Understanding J. Gresham Machen

A CONTROVERSIAL LEGACY

J. GRESHAM MACHEN (1881-1937) was not a typical fundamentalist or evangelical. He belonged to one of the subgroups, strict Presbyterians loyal to the Old Princeton theology that looked to the Westminster Confession of Faith for its creed. He did not like being called a fundamentalist, he was an intellectual, he was ill-at-ease with the emotionalism and oversimplifications of revival meetings, he opposed church involvement in politics including even the widely popular Prohibition movement, and he declined to join in the antievolution crusade. Yet he was willing to make common cause with popular fundamentalism. In his view modernist theology threatened to undermine Christianity by proclaiming another gospel. His volume *Christianity and Liberalism* (1923) cast him as the foremost spokesperson for the fundamentalist coalition.

During the following years Machen became the leading controversialist in the (northern) Presbyterian Church in the U.S.A. After efforts to oust modernists from Presbyterian pulpits had failed by 1926, liberals and moderates launched a counterattack. Machen, a New Testament scholar at Princeton Theological Seminary, was refused a promotion at the seminary, following an investigation of his divisiveness by a committee of the General Assembly of the Presbyterian Church. Furthermore, the General Assembly reorganized the seminary to wrest control from the conservatives. This led Machen to leave Princeton in 1929 to found Westminster Theological Seminary in Philadelphia.

Alarmed that modernism, rather than the traditional evangelical message of salvation through the atoning work of Christ alone, was being proclaimed by the foreign missionaries of the Presbyterian Church in the U.S.A., Machen founded in 1933 the Independent Board for Presbyterian Foreign Missions. The denomination responded in 1935 by defrocking Machen from the ministry on the grounds that he had defied church authority. Machen and a few thousand followers left to found their own denomination in 1936; but his death early the next year left a small and struggling movement.

Despite Machen's apparent failure in these immediate church battles, his broader work continued after his death to have a major impact on fundamentalism and evangelicalism. Three of his students, Harold Ockenga, Carl McIntire, and Francis Schaeffer, for instance, were instrumental in shaping some of the most pivotal later movements. If we consider the many others who were influenced by these men, we can include Billy Graham, who worked closely in many organizations with Ockenga, and Jerry Falwell, who was influenced in important ways by Schaeffer. Many other lines of influence can be traced as well. Several of the leading conservative evangelical theological seminaries, including Westminster, Faith, Fuller, Covenant, Gordon-Conwell, and Reformed, counted Machen as one of their models. During the academic dark age of conservative evangelicalism, from the 1920s through the 1940s, Machen was the major counterexample against the accusation that the movement was incompatible with serious scholarship. The intellectual renaissance beginning with the rise of neo-evangelicalism in the 1950s was inspired in part by Machen's example.[1]

1. Cf. George Marsden, *Reforming Fundamentalism: Fuller Seminary and the New Evangelicalism* (Grand Rapids: Eerdmans, 1987).

Yet Machen remained controversial, and even many evangelical scholars repudiated his heritage. The most notorious example came in 1959 when Edward J. Carnell, president of Fuller Theological Seminary, devoted a chapter in his volume *The Case for Orthodox Theology*[2] to the "cultic mentality" of Machen. Repudiations of Machen's narrowness have been frequent since then. Almost all evangelical scholars who are not strictly Reformed have found his Presbyterian confessionalism too narrow, and even many of the strictly Reformed have rejected his Princetonian apologetics for Kuyperian models, or have been unhappy with his insistence on ecclesiastical separatism.

If Machen's image has suffered among his friends, it surely has not improved from its subzero rating among the heirs of his former enemies. In mainline Protestant circles Machen's name is about as popular as would be J. Edgar Hoover's at a meeting of the ACLU. He is seen as simply a troublemaker and a narrow bigoted crank.

The purpose of this chapter is to develop a more sympathetic understanding of Machen even while conceding some of the points made by his critics. In so doing we are considering one instance of a larger question in evaluating fundamentalism and evangelicalism. A crucial dimension of these movements is that they have been willing to take a stand against twentieth-century theological innovation that they see as changing the nature of the gospel. Each instance in which such a stand has been taken has been shaped by particularities of personality, church setting, and peculiar American traditions, any one of which might lead us to dismiss the stand entirely. On the other hand, a contrasting approach is to ask, once we have taken into account such peculiarities that shape each individual's decisions, how we should evaluate the stance in terms of larger issues and trends?

2. Edward J. Carnell, *The Case for Orthodox Theology* (Philadelphia: Westminster Press, 1959), pp. 113-26. Cf. Marsden, *Reforming Fundamentalism*, pp. 188-92.

INTERPRETATIONS OF MACHEN

Any historical person or movement must be understood at a number of levels. Yet the tendency of historical interpretation, especially of controversial subjects, is to reduce our interpretation to just one level. In the case of J. Gresham Machen, we can see these reductionist tendencies in the interpretations both of his strongest supporters and of his sharpest detractors.

Supporters of Machen tend to interpret him simply at the level of the doctrine for which he stood. This level of interpretation clearly is of immense importance. Machen stood in the Old School Old Princeton doctrinal tradition. He was heir to the tradition of Charles Hodge and B. B. Warfield, and was in fact a protégé of the latter. His controversialism was not unlike theirs, not unlike Hodge's in helping to exclude the mildly innovative New School Party from the Presbyterian Church in 1837, not unlike Warfield's militant opposition to Charles Briggs's questioning of the inerrancy of Scripture in the 1890s. This was a venerable heritage, and Machen owned it entirely. His predecessors presumably would have done much the same.

According to this view, understanding Machen is a matter of understanding the tradition and the issues. The questions were simply matters of principle. Machen recognized that modernism had crept into the Presbyterian church. As he argued in *Christianity and Liberalism* (1923) liberal theology was not merely a variation within the Christian tradition like the New School theology. It was, Machen insisted, another religion, since it proposed an entirely new view of Jesus and a scheme of salvation other than Christianity had ever taught before. Having worked to purge the denomination of liberalism, Machen became convinced that the denomination and Princeton Seminary after its reorganization were irreversibly committed to tolerance. Tolerance of modernism, Machen was convinced, was incompatible with a true church, even if most of the tolerant people were themselves otherwise conservative. So as a man of Old School principle, having failed to purge the church, Machen felt forced to leave.

185

There is a good bit to be said for this view. It explains much of what happened.[3] What it does not explain very well is why Machen went on a course that eventually left him almost alone among his contemporaries. Although a few younger people followed him, by the time he organized what became the Orthodox Presbyterian Church in 1936, the path he had taken had been forsaken by some of the staunchest of his Old School allies, most notably Clarence Macartney, the other major figure in the conservative efforts of the 1920s to purge the church of modernism.

The other common interpretation of Machen goes to the opposite extreme and is popular among his detractors. According to these interpreters the bitter controversies at Princeton Seminary and Machen's later struggles against the Presbyterian Church in the U.S.A. can be explained largely in terms of Machen's personality. This was one of the explanations offered at the time. When the majority of the committee for the General Assembly of 1926 recommended against his promotion at Princeton, they cited among other things his "temperamental idiosyncrasies."[4] Both at the time and since critics of Machen have suggested that there was something peculiar about him. Most often mentioned are that Machen remained a bachelor and his very close relationship to his mother until her death in 1931. Neither of these traits, however, was particularly unusual in the Victorian era, which certainly set many of Machen's social standards.

More to the point is that he does seem to have had a flaring temper and a propensity to make strong remarks about individuals with whom he disagreed. One striking instance is from 1913 when Machen had an intense two-hour argument with B. B. Warfield over campus policy, after which Machen wrote to his mother that Warfield, whom he normally admired

3. Daryl G. Hart argues very intelligently for this view in " 'Doctor Fundamentalis': An Intellectual Biography of J. Gresham Machen, 1881-1937" (Ph.D. dissertation, The Johns Hopkins University, 1988).

4. Ned B. Stonehouse, *J. Gresham Machen: A Biographical Memoir* (Grand Rapids: Eerdmans, 1954), p. 389.

immensely, was "himself, despite some very good qualities, a very heartless, selfish, domineering sort of man."[5] You can imagine that, if someone says things like this about one's friends, that it might be easy to make enemies. Machen does not seem to have had a great ability to separate people from issues, and this certainly added to the tensions on the small seminary faculty. Clearly he was someone whom people either loved or hated. His students disciples were charmed by him and always spoke of his warmth and gentlemanliness. His opponents found him impossible, and it is a fair question to ask whether, despite the serious issues, things might have gone differently with a different personality involved.

So, I think that each of these levels for understanding Machen has some merit and perhaps they can be balanced against each other in some way. However, I do not propose to explore them any further here. Rather I want to look at two other levels for understanding Machen that are less on the surface and less controversial, but which may throw light on him regardless of whether one sees him as a twentieth-century Martin Luther standing up for the faith or as a crank.

HISTORY AND TRUTH

One key to understanding Machen is to look at the philosophical assumptions that lay beneath his theology and his controversialism.[6] Particularly interesting is his view of history. The problem of history has arguably been *the* twentieth-century problem. For many people, all absolutes have been dissolved in historical relativism.

Machen was acutely aware of this problem and frequently returned to the point that Christianity was a "historical" re-

5. J. Gresham Machen to Mary Gresham Machen, 5 October 1913 and 12 October 1913, Machen papers, Westminster Theological Seminary.

6. The following section is a substantial revision of George M. Marsden, "J. Gresham Machen, History, and Truth," *Westminster Theological Journal* 42/1 (Fall 1979), 157-75. Some of the sentences are the same.

ligion, that is, it was based on historical events that actually happened, or it was nothing.

This question was intensely personal to Machen and reflected his own deep intellectual crisis as a young man. Reared in rigorous Old School Presbyterianism, Machen was nonetheless educated at Johns Hopkins, the cradle of modern American academia. After completing his B.D. at Princeton Theological Seminary, he spent 1905-6 in Germany. There he was directly exposed to the theological implications of modern historical consciousness and of higher criticism. He was especially enamored of the theology and piety of Wilhelm Herrman, with whom he studied at Marburg.

Meanwhile, his mother, an extraordinarily intelligent person herself, was writing impassioned pleas not be to taken in by the new scholarship. Machen replied with very uncharacteristic indignation. His parents, he said, were asking him to believe in something without a thorough investigation of its intellectual merits. It is, he wrote, "a purely *intellectual* question, a question of fact, before me of settlement. What it demands," he said, is a "a perfectly free, impartial examination. . . ."[7]

Machen's Princeton mentor, William P. Armstrong, prevailed on Machen to return the next year as an instructor in Greek, perhaps as part of a concerted effort to rescue a young man who showed all the signs of moving toward liberal Christianity. Machen accepted, but only with the strongest protests about his unsuitability for the position. He accepted it only with the assurance from Armstrong that he would have to sign no theological pledge nor do more than "stand on the broad principles of the Reformed Theology."[8] To his mother he wrote that "Nobody ever started a work with more misgivings," and then, as though to say she had not won, he added, "of course

7. J. Gresham Machen to Mary Gresham Machen, September 14, 1906, quoted in Stonehouse, *J. Gresham Machen*, pp. 139-40.
8. William P. Armstrong to J. Gresham Machen, July 14, 1906, quoted in Stonehouse, *J. Gresham Machen*, p. 133.

intellectually I shall be living to a greater extent in Germany than I was last year."[9] Although Machen's firm intention had been to leave Princeton after one year to prepare for another profession,[10] he stayed on as an instructor, and after a few years was brought back safely into the Old School fold.

Nonetheless, Machen remained thoroughly committed to the project outlined in his letter to his mother from Germany, the project of proving whether Christianity was historically true. "Must we stake our salvation upon the intricacies of historical research?" he asked in his inaugural address in 1915, upon becoming an Assistant Professor in New Testament. Machen's autobiographical answer clearly was "Yes." "If the Bible *were* false, your faith would go." "The sacredness of history," he said in another place, ". . . does not prevent it from being history; and if it is history, it should be studied by the best historical method which can be attained."[11]

Machen's major scholarly works, *The Origin of Paul's Religion* (1921) and *The Virgin Birth of Christ* (1930) both are monuments to careful historical research and argumentation. Each attempts to demonstrate the hypothesis that the traditional supernaturalistic biblical claims better explain the evidence than do competing naturalistic accounts.

Clearly a major difference between Machen's approach and most modern historical scholarship is that Machen did not a priori rule out supernaturalistic or miraculous explanations. Rather, he started out with the hypothesis that biblical claims should be taken at face value and then argued that this hypothesis better explained the facts than any other.

Beyond that, however, was a more subtle difference be-

9. J. Gresham Machen to Mary Gresham Machen, September 11, 1906, quoted in Stonehouse, *J. Gresham Machen*, p. 137.

10. Stonehouse, *J. Gresham Machen*, p. 145.

11. "History and Faith," in Machen, *What is Christianity and Other Addresses*, ed. Ned B. Stonehouse (Grand Rapids: Eerdmans, 1951), p. 170; W. John Cook, ed., *The New Testament: An Introduction to its Literature and History* (Edinburgh: Banner of Truth Trust, 1976), p. 9 (originally published as Sunday-school materials ca. 1916).

tween Machen and most other twentieth-century historians. This difference was that they had differing understandings of what historians did, particularly differing views of the relationships between facts and interpretation.

We can understand Machen's views better by setting them against those of almost the extreme opposite, the views of Carl Becker, who I think was the most profound spokesman for the most modern views of the era. Becker was essentially a pragmatist. He held, along with other pragmatists, that our minds organize reality for our own purposes, but that we have no way of knowing whether our experiences correspond to anything outside of ourselves. "Truth" is a social construct of what works in our time and place.

In 1931 Becker delivered to the American Historical Association a very influential presidential address entitled "Everyman His Own Historian." The starting point for his argument was that, although events in the past no doubt occurred, they now exist for us only as ideas that we hold in our memories. History then is only the *memory* of the past. It is not the past itself, which is forever gone. So the only place that George Washington exists is in our collective memories. We do not know George Washington himself, but only various *interpretations* of him that survive—his interpretations of himself, his contemporaries' interpretations, and the interpretations of later historians and others. Our views of the past, then, "will inevitably be a blend of fact and fancy." Historians then are in the business of "the keeping of the useful myths" of society. Hence, historians are dealing not so much with facts as with socially constructed interpretations. (One can recognize almost all the major themes of contemporary hermeneutics in Becker's 1931 address.) So, said Becker, the old idea of using scientific means to discover the fixed facts of history was an illusion. Rather, what were considered "the facts" varied with the time, the place, and the perspective of the historians. To set forth historical facts, said Becker, was not like "dumping a barrow of bricks."

Machen had an entirely different view of fact than did

Becker. "There is one good thing about facts," said Machen, —they stay put." (Machen did not see himself as dumping his barrow, but otherwise he might have affirmed just the image Becker was rejecting.) "If a thing really happened," Machen goes on, "the passage of years can never possibly make it into a thing that did not happen." Becker, on the other hand, reserved this changeless quality for the now-past *events* that presumably happened. "Facts," however, in any practical sense meant our memories of these now-inaccessible events. Not only did Becker say, "left to themselves, the facts do not speak"; he added, "left to themselves, they do not exist, not really, since for all practical purposes there is no fact until someone affirms it."[12] Machen said just the opposite. "The facts of the Christian religion remain facts no matter whether we cherish them or not: they are facts for God; they are facts both for angels and for demons; they are facts now, and they will remain facts beyond the end of time."[13]

It would be difficult to find a clearer contrast between the hermeneutical views that have come to prevail in the twentieth century and those characteristic of earlier eras.

Machen even went so far as to deny the view of Becker, and of many Americans of his day, that facts (or events in Becker's sense) were properly open to a variety of interpretations, each of which might be valid in relation to its time, place, and point of view. Machen regarded events as inherently having a fixed significance—that significance they had in the eyes of God. So in order to know a fact, we need also to discover its significance. In the case of scriptural events this significance is revealed by God himself. In any case the significance of facts is not dependent on an interpretation that we impose on it and hence subject to change. Rather, what we do in historical interpretation is to attempt to *discover* the true facts and their significance. Humans do not create meaning, they find it.

12. Carl Becker, *Everyman His Own Historian: Essays on History and Politics* (Chicago: Quadrangle Books, 1966 [1935]), pp. 233-55.
13. Machen, *What is Faith?* (New York: Macmillan, 1925), p. 249.

So insistent was Machen that the human mind should not *impose* its categories on reality, but rather discover the truth that was already there, that he took exception to the modern use of the word "interpretation." "I hesitate to use the word 'interpretation,'" he told the students at the opening exercises for Westminster Seminary in 1929, "for it is a word that has been the custodian of more nonsense, perhaps, than any other word in the English language today."[14]

Machen's philosophical and hermeneutical views may sound quaint among many avant-garde academics sixty years later; but sixty years earlier they would have been commonplace at most American academic institutions. Essentially Machen's views reflected the teachings of Scottish Common Sense Realism, which had dominated American academic thought through the Civil War era. Machen does not seem to have referred to Scottish Common Sense philosophy directly, but he often appealed more generally to "common sense" in opposition to modern thought[15] and he certainly shared the assumptions of Scottish philosophy first introduced at Princeton by John Witherspoon.[16]

Common Sense Realism asserted, as indeed most people seem to believe, that the human mind is so constructed that the real world can be the direct object of our thought. In some important sense, we perceive what is actually there. Philosophers, especially since Locke, however, had interposed between us and the real world the concept of ideas. These ideas, they said, were the real objects of our thought; hence we do not know anything at a distance, but only in our minds. Thomas Reid (1710-1796), the principal formulator of Scottish Realism, responded that the doctrine of ideas would only lead to skepticism as it already had for his countryman, David Hume. Everyone in fact does believe, said Reid, that a real

14. "Westminster Theological Seminary: Its Purpose and Plan," *What is Christianity?*, p. 226. Cf. *What is Faith?*, pp. 145-46.

15. See Marsden, "J. Gresham Machen," p. 165n.

16. On this background see Mark A. Noll, *Princeton and the Republic: 1768-1822* (Princeton: Princeton University Press, 1989).

world exists and that we can know something about it. The only people who have ever doubted this are philosophers and madmen. When philosophers attempt to deny such common-sense beliefs, says Reid, it is like people walking on their hands. Once we stop looking at them, they get down and live like the rest of us. So Humeans duck when they go through low door-ways.[17]

Common Sense views are relevant to our contrasting views of history. Carl Becker's view is clearly an extension of the principle of the primacy of ideas as what we know, com-bined with the post-Kantian belief that the mind functions to impose its categories and in some sense, then, creates reality as we can know it. Machen's views, on the other hand, reflect Common Sense philosophy. One of the things taught by Com-mon Sense philosophy was that we can know something about the past just as we can know things about the present world. "That there is such a city as Rome," said Reid, "I am as certain of as any proposition of Euclid. . . ."[18] So with historical knowl-edge. Based on the right sorts of reliable evidence, we can establish probabilities as to what happened in the past. And if the evidence is good enough, we are justified in believing these facts with virtual certainty. So I can be certain that Julius Caesar lived. Such a fact is, in itself, not a matter of interpretation. Everyone already believes such views of knowledge, says Reid. Courts of law settle matters of life and death on just such evidence from reliable testimony from the past.

One can appreciate, then, why Machen, holding to this commonsense view of truth, would have faced such a serious crisis in his own life when confronted with higher criticism of the Bible, and why, once having committed himself to the traditional faith, would see the historical investigation of the facts of the matter as so crucial to the defense of twentieth-

17. S. A. Grave, *The Scottish Philosophy of Common Sense* (Oxford: Oxford University Press, 1960), esp. pp. 11-28; Thomas Reid, "Essays on the Intellectual Powers of Man" (1785), in William Hamilton, ed., *The Works of Thomas Reid,* fifth ed. (Edinburgh, 1858), passim.
18. Reid, "Intellectual Powers," p. 166.

century Christianity. Machen's father and maternal grand-father were lawyers, and Machen took the same common-sensical view toward the issue of the truth or falsity of the historical claims of Christianity. Either traditional Christianity was true to the facts and historical investigation would confirm it, or Christianity's traditional historical claims as to who Jesus was and what he had done were false. In that case one should face up to the facts and abandon the claim to be Christian. Modernist theologies, said Machen, were evading this simple commonsense issue with fancy language about interpretation and the like. Hence they should be exposed for what they were and for denying simple claims as to matters of fact that Christians in every other generation had made.

A SOUTHERN PERSPECTIVE

We will come back to some of the implications of this outlook. But first let us look briefly at an entirely different level for understanding Machen. This level of interpretation has to do with the fact that Machen, like a number of people associated with the fundamentalist movement, was a Southerner. (For what I say here I am very largely dependent on the work of my colleague, Bradley Longfield, who has provided a valuable collective biographical account of Machen and other leaders in the 1920s fundamentalist vs. modernist controversies in the Presbyterian Church in the U.S.A.)[19]

J. Gresham Machen's father, Arthur Machen (1826-1915), although reared in Washington, D.C., and practicing law in Baltimore, was a Southerner by heritage and in his sympathies. During the War Between the States he declined a position as Attorney General of Maryland, lest he might have

19. Bradley James Longfield, *The Presbyterian Controversy: Fundamentalists, Modernists, and Moderates* (New York: Oxford University Press, 1991). See also his "The Presbyterian Controversy, 1922-1936: Christianity, Culture, and Ecclesiastical Conflict" (Ph.D. dissertation, Duke University, 1988), from which the following citations are taken.

to prosecute other Confederate sympathizers. In 1863 he moved to the Franklin Street Presbyterian Church, a congregation of southern sympathies that, as soon as the war was over, joined the Southern Presbyterian Church. (The Presbyterian Church in the U.S.A. separated in 1861 from its northern counterpart.) In 1873 Arthur Machen (a bachelor until he was 47, by the way) married the considerably younger Mary Gresham.

Mary Gresham Machen was indelibly a daughter of the Lost Cause. Born in 1849, she grew up during the war in Macon, Georgia, where her father, John Gresham (1818-1891), was a prominent attorney and one of the staunchest of Old School Presbyterians. Mary's brother served in the Confederate army. While Baltimore was considered almost a southern city, Mary Machen's heart was always deeper in Dixie. As a matter of course, she was an active member of the United Daughters of the Confederacy.

J. Gresham Machen shared his family's southern aristocratic sympathies throughout his life. Regarding the Confederacy, he wrote to a correspondent in 1925 that he was convinced the southern states "were acting in the plainest possible exercise of constitutional rights, and that the real revolution was entered into by those who endeavored to prevent such plainly guaranteed rights."[20] He also shared southern attitudes toward race, combining affirmations that blacks could represent "the best part of human nature"[21] with the most adamant insistence that blacks and whites should remain socially separated. In fact, the matter mentioned earlier that he was so furious at Warfield about in 1913 was the seminary's permission to allow a black student to reside in the dormitories in which Machen had a room. (Warfield, interestingly, was a progressive on the race question, coming from the side of the Kentucky Breckinridges who supported the Union.) Machen's attitude was not un-

20. Longfield, p. 89n.
21. Longfield, p. 69.

195

usual in the context of the day; for instance, in 1922 President Lowell of Harvard refused to let black students live in its dorms and Princeton University did not have a black graduate until 1947.[22] Nonetheless, Machen's vehemence on the point illustrates his strongly southern attitudes.

Ecclesiastically, Machen did not leave the southern church for the northern until 1913, when it was required in order that he might become an assistant professor. In the southern church, of course, Old School theology and the attendant commonsense philosophy continued to reign long after they were put on the defensive in the North.

Machen's southern loyalties cast light on his political views, which were radically libertarian. He opposed almost any extension of state power and took stands on a variety of issues. Like most libertarians, his stances violated usual categories of liberal and conservative. For instance, he opposed child labor legislation, but also opposed Prohibition. He was against national parks and even went so far as to oppose an ordinance against jaywalking in Philadelphia. On the other hand, consistent with his libertarian principles, he opposed the Lusk laws in New York state that would have required state licenses for all nonpublic schools, arguing that the laws' supposed usefulness for checking radicalism was misguided. Only by preserving free speech, he said, was there hope for the one instrument that could stop radicalism. "That instrument is reasonable persuasion."[23]

Machen's stance against Prohibition cost him in his ecclesiastical struggles, especially in 1926 when the Presbyterian General Assembly was considering his promotion at Princeton. At the time, support of Prohibition was virtually an article of faith among both progressives and conservatives in mainline

22. David O. Levine, *The American College and the Culture of Aspiration, 1915-1940* (Ithaca: Cornell University Press, 1986), p. 159; Marcia Graham Synott, *The Half-Opened Door: Discrimination and Admissions at Harvard, Yale, and Princeton, 1900-1970* (Westport, CN: Greenwod Press, 1979), pp. 160-98, 218-25.

23. Stonehouse, *J. Gresham Machen*, p. 403; cf. pp. 401-8.

denominations, and Machen's contrary views apparently were used against him.[24]

When asked why he would not allow as much liberty in the church as he would in the state, Machen replied that the church was a voluntary organization and hence had a perfect right to insist on its own constitutional rules.[25] Nonetheless, within the context of his Old School heritage, which included a strong view of the church's authority, Machen always reserved a considerable place for the rights of the individual. In *Christianity and Liberalism,* published in 1923 when it still seemed that conservatives might be a majority, Machen suggested that liberals should, in honesty, simply leave the church if they did not agree with its constitution. He regarded himself as having similar individual rights. First, he forsook Old School tradition for New School practice by establishing an independent seminary and then the Independent Board for Presbyterian Foreign Missions. When he was defrocked for establishing the rival board, he felt perfectly free to leave and found his own denomination. As Bradley Longfield suggests, having been reared in a congregation which left the northern church for the southern, for Machen secession "provided not only an acceptable, but in many respects an honorable, solution to irreconcilable disagreements of principle."[26]

EVALUATIONS

It is not difficult to find elements of Machen's commonsense philosophy and of his southernness with which one might disagree. When we do so, though, I think we should be careful not to dismiss all his views just because we have identified their sources. That would be the genetic fallacy—to think you have refuted a view by finding its origins. Since all our views have origins, they all stand on equal ground in that regard.

24. Ibid., pp. 483-84.
25. Machen, *What is Christianity?*, pp. 113-14.
26. Longfield, "The Presbyterian Controversy," p. 122.

Many readers may also disagree with the militant and ultimately separatist stances Machen took. Nonetheless, it may still be useful to suggest a few aspects of his outlook that, even so, Christians from somewhat different traditions might find illuminating and useful.

First regarding Common Sense philosophy: as I have argued elsewhere,[27] I believe it led Machen to overestimate the prowess of rational argument and underestimate the importance of point of view. Nonetheless, I also think that it helped Machen recognize some trends that few other mainline Protestant thinkers seemed worried about at the time. Particularly, Machen recognized that modern hermeneutics was on a track leading toward what we have today. Some of this is, I think, fairly designated as—to use Machen's term—nonsense. For instance, this seems to me to be a fair term for some of the radical deconstruction that is the current fashion. As I understand it—and I suppose that I am free to interpret it any way I want—it asserts as an absolute that we cannot get beyond our own interpretations and therefore there are no absolutes. Although this view may be the most consistent result of assuming a purely naturalistic chance universe, it seems to me incompatible with anything like a traditional Christian view. Just as a twentieth-century historian I appreciate the importance of the many lenses through which we view reality, so as a Christian I think it is necessary to build our accounts of reality around premises that include the affirmation that God has created both our minds and the rest of the world. That starting point has important implications for our epistemology. Furthermore, it seems to me nonnegotiable for Christians to believe that God has revealed himself historically, especially in the Incarnation, and hence we must be able to learn something about reality through history and texts outside of ourselves.[28]

27. Marsden, "J. Gresham Machen," pp. 157-75.
28. I have discussed these points further in "The Spiritual Vision of History," in C. T. McIntire and Ronald A. Wells, eds., *History and His-*

If Common Sense philosophy, early nineteenth-century American academics, and people like Machen went too far in one extreme on such issues, popular academic opinion today, it seems to me, has gone too far to the other extreme. Machen can remind us that it might not be a bad idea for Christians to stop trying to suit current academic fads and to see if there is anything that distinguishes their philosophical outlook basically from prevailing modern ones.

Finally, Machen as a Southerner may have something to offer us. As a Southerner Machen was an outsider to the mainline Protestant establishment and hence may again have been alert to important trends that others were not seeing. Particularly, I think we can see these insights in a convocation address he gave in 1912, later published as "Christianity and Culture." In it, Machen emphasized the importance of the intellectual task in the confrontation of Christianity and modern culture. Probably he overestimated the degree to which the task of the church in the twentieth century should be an intellectual one. On the other hand, I am convinced that he was right that many of his Christian contemporaries were underestimating the intellectual crisis they faced. Reflecting his own intense personal tensions when studying in the advanced intellectual atmosphere of Germany, Machen was acutely sensitive to the way prevailing academic opinion could undermine Christianity. "We may preach with all the fervor of a reformer," he declared in his 1912 address, "and yet succeed only in winning a straggler here and there, if we permit the whole collective thought of the nation or of the world to be controlled by ideas which, by the resistless force of logic, prevent Christianity from being regarded as anything more than a harmless delusion." In Machen's view, academic debates ultimately had profound practical consequences. "What is to-day matter of academic spec-

---

torical Understanding (Grand Rapids: Eerdmans, 1981), and in "Evangelicals, History, and Modernity," in George Marsden, ed., *Evangelicals and Modern America* (Grand Rapids: Eerdmans, 1984).

ulation, begins to-morrow to move armies and pull down empires."[29]

This insight—which I think is a profound one—does not seem to have been compelling to many American Protestant leaders, either liberal, moderate, or conservative, in the first half of the twentieth century. In fact, just at the time when Machen spoke, the American Protestant establishment was in the process of abandoning almost all the distinctly Christian elements of the vast network of universities it controlled. There were many reasons—some of them good—for this secularization of American universities. Nonetheless, the outcome, which we can see today in that mainline Protestants have almost nothing to show in the field of higher education, is one that is at least puzzling—especially given the long tradition of Protestant involvement in higher education.

Machen, in part because he was an outsider and one trained in commonsense categories, attempted to sound an alarm about this trend that few of his peers were prepared to hear.

In some areas, at least, then, perhaps we might view Machen's role as analogous to that of some other outsiders of the era who because of their distinctive experience saw things in ways that others did not. Perhaps some of the southern literary figures of the era are analogous. Or in the field of religion, the closest counterparts may be the Niebuhr brothers, Reinhold and H. Richard, who in part because they were reared in the German-speaking Evangelical Synod were alert to issues of Christianity and culture that persons raised within the establishment were less likely to see.

J. Gresham Machen—especially as a commonsense theologian and as a Southerner—in some ways might be considered a period piece. Not only that, he might be considered a somewhat cantankerous period piece. He had a personality that only his good friends found appealing, and he stood for

29. J. Gresham Machen, "Christianity and Culture," *Princeton Theological Review* 11 (1913), 7.

a narrow Old School confessionalism and exclusivism that many people today find appalling.

Nonetheless, despite all these features which might tempt us to dismiss him, I think we can also see that here also was a deeply committed Christian of great insight. Even from the point of view of mainline Protestantism, it seems that at least it must be conceded that much of what he said about liberal Christianity and of the dangers of accommodation to the standards of twentieth-century liberal culture anticipated the neo-orthodox critique of the same things. Or, more precisely, it paralleled Karl Barth's critique of modernism, which appeared at almost the same moment, just after World War I. In fact, though neither would have appreciated the comparison, there are some striking parallels between Machen and Barth. The most striking is that both were thoroughly captivated for a time by the personality, piety, and theological power of Wilhelm Herrmann, with whom they studied at Marburg just two years apart.[30] Later they each turned from Herrmann in differing degrees. Nonetheless, despite the obvious vast differences, there were also some parallel insights they offered in their assessments of liberal theology and liberal culture. Perhaps the chief reason for these parallels was that each subjected twentieth-century modernism to the light of Scripture and found modernism wanting.

Not everyone, of course, will agree with that judgment. Though the old modernism of the 1920s is now largely defunct, new postmodernisms have risen to take its place. Those who do not find in such developments the hope of the world may be grateful to persons such as Machen and many others who, whatever their faults, insisted that traditional Christianity still had an important role to play in the twentieth century.

---

30. Barth said, "Herrmann was *the* theological teacher of my student years"; Eberhard Busch, *Karl Barth: His Life from Letters and Autobiographical Texts*, trans. John Bowden (Philadelphia: Fortress Press, 1976), p. 44.

Index

202